Transformed
by Pastoral Transition

A Guide for
Congregations

MARCIA B. BAILEY

FOREWORD BY NORMAN B. BENDROTH

JUDSON PRESS
PUBLISHERS SINCE 1824
VALLEY FORGE, PA

Transformed by Pastoral Transition: A Guide for Congregations
© 2021 by Judson Press, Valley Forge, PA 19482-0851
All rights reserved.

Judson Press has made every effort to trace the ownership of all quotes. In the event of a question arising from the use of a quote, we regret any error made and will be pleased to make the necessary correction in future printings and editions of this book.

Bible quotations in this volume are from the New Revised Standard Version of the Bible, copyright © 1989 by the Division of Christian Education of the National Council of the Churches of Christ in the United States of America. Used by permission. All rights reserved.

Permission granted from both Randolph Miller, President, Ministers Council ABCUSA and C. Jeff Woods, Acting General Secretary, ABCUSA, for the inclusion of Transition Ministries ABCUSA Code of Ethics and The Covenant and Code of Ethics.

Interior design by Crystal Devine.
Cover design by Wendy Ronga, Hampton Design Group.

Library of Congress Cataloging-in-Publication data

Names: Bailey, Marcia B., author.
Title: Transformed by pastoral transition : a guide for congregations /
    Marcia B. Bailey.
Description: Valley Forge, PA : Judson Press, 2021. | Includes
    bibliographical references
Identifiers: LCCN 2020033803 (print) | LCCN 2020033804 (ebook) | ISBN
    9780817018207 (paperback) | ISBN 9780817082215 (epub)
Subjects: LCSH: Christian leadership. | Change--Religious
    aspects--Christianity. | Clergy--Relocation.
Classification: LCC BV652.1 .B36 2021 (print) | LCC BV652.1 (ebook) | DDC
    254--dc23
LC record available at https://lccn.loc.gov/2020033803
LC ebook record available at https://lccn.loc.gov/2020033804

Printed in the U.S.A.

First printing, 2021.

CONTENTS

Foreword   *iv*

Preface   *vi*

Prelude   *vii*

Chapters

1   Call to Worship   *1*

2   Invocation   *21*

3   The "Not Just for Kids" Conversation   *33*

4   Special Music   *61*

5   The Word in Words   *74*

6   Offering   *90*

7   Communion   *109*

8   Hymn of Expectation   *129*

9   Benediction   *140*

Postlude: The Appendices

A   A Congregational Debrief   *143*

B   Five Focus Areas for Transition Ministry   *148*

C   Transition Ministries ABCUSA Code of Ethics
    and The Covenant and Code of Ethics   *151*

D   Lectio Divina   *155*

E   A Transitional Sermon   *156*

FOREWORD

I have been an intentional interim minister for more than 25 years. I have served 11 churches as an interim pastor, served on the faculty of the Interim Ministry Network, and wrote two books on the practice of interim ministry. *Transformed by Pastoral Transition* by Marcia B. Bailey is a volume I wish I had had to pass along to anxious parishioners as they entered a time of transition. William Bridges rightly points out that change, per se, is not what makes people uneasy, but transitions do—that in-between-time when you are betwixt new pastors and new circumstances. Rev. Bailey has written a guidebook to help church members navigate these choppy, emotional waters.

Transformed by Pastoral Transition addresses the existential, emotional, and spiritual challenges that parishioners are likely to face during a time of transition, instead of being a "how-to" book about the process. The book's title is the theme that runs throughout: transition is a time for transformation, not to hunker down or ride it out. Bailey speaks perceptively about the difference between being "broken" and being "broken open." We may feel broken by trauma or grief at a pastor's departure, but the circumstances provide an opportunity to be broken open, to make room for the Holy Spirit to challenge, teach, and transform us during this time.

Dr. Bailey is well-qualified to write such a book. As a seasoned pastor, intentional interim minister, and educator, she has seen warts, wrinkles, and beauty marks that all churches and congregations exhibit. She is well-attuned to the particular needs and opportunities that communities of faith experience during times of disruption. Bailey draws on the interdisciplinary insights of others to inform her own work with local churches, applying Margaret Wheatly's thinking about systems and theories of change to congregational capacity to self-organize in times of chaos, and using William Bridges' wisdom about institutional transitions to inform her observations about how churches experience endings, in-between-times, and new beginnings.

This volume is helpfully organized as if it were a Sunday church service. Each chapter is titled an element of worship, from the Prelude to the Benediction. This device effectively sets the context for ministry in times of transition. Though unsettling, such a time is surrounded by God's guiding grace and thus may become an act of worship. Each chapter uses its liturgical title to address the work ahead: for example, Call to Worship invites us to explore what are we called to do and become; Invocation opens us to discern where we need to ask for help; Offering calls us to offer safe space, leadership, and understanding for people. The chapters are fleshed out with good pastoral care, sound biblical examples, and helpful advice for ministry.

Each chapter concludes with Takeaways, which remind the reader of the key learnings from the chapter and provide a helpful summary, and Congregational Resources, which include prayers, liturgical resources, and questions for individual and group consideration. The appendices have additional practical tools for congregations in transition.

This book is what I would put into the hands of a pastoral search committee, a transition team, and any other church leaders or parishioners who are anxious to learn more about the transition time. It will surely be a source of comfort, inspiration, and guidance to all who read it and benefit from Rev. Bailey's wisdom.

—REV. NORMAN B. BENDROTH, DMIN
Author, *Interim Ministry in Action:*
A Handbook for Churches in Transition
Editor, *Transitional Ministry Today:*
Successful Strategies for Churches and Pastors
church-consultants.org

PREFACE

I began writing this book in my head several years ago as I worked with congregations experiencing a pastoral transition. Serving as either their transitional pastor or as a regional consultant, I spoke with church folks who were sad, worried, conflicted, relieved, hopeful, or uncertain about the season of change that lay before them. I could find few helpful resources to give them.

Fortunately, Judson Press also realized the need, and together we hope this book provides congregations with a clear understanding and possibilities for direct action to make the season of transition a time of congregational transformation. My thanks to Judson Press publisher, Laura Alden, and editor, Rebecca Irwin-Diehl, for their enthusiasm and encouragement.

I began to write the manuscript in January 2020 and was deep into the process when, on March 15, those of us in Pennsylvania were ordered to stay at home for the next several weeks of the COVID-19 pandemic. One of the things I have had to do during this time, besides writing and making face masks, is to transition my own congregation to online worship, meetings, and study. Many of the activities that are provided for you in this book assume in-person gatherings; feel free to adapt them to whatever situation you find yourselves in. I have offered some suggestions throughout the book for virtual engagement. The purpose behind the gathering or conversation is what is most important.

Finally, my deepest thanks to the individuals and congregations who have allowed me to accompany them on their own journeys through transition; they have been my teachers, and I have learned much about the possibility of being transformed by pastoral transition from them.

PRELUDE

PREPARING TO THRIVE

While many books are available to help the transitioning pastor, few are directed toward the experience and needs of the transitioning congregation. This book is intended to speak to where you find yourselves, what you might be feeling, and how you might move forward, and to do so with the recognition that this time of transition might be a season of transformation in the life of your congregation. While change might be hard, it can also be good. While the way may not be automatically clear, it can be discovered. How we navigate change, how we think about it and experience it, makes all the difference in whether we see change as a negative or positive experience in our lives. Seasons of pastoral change, of leadership transition, are no different.

> *Within the saying goodbye and the letting go, amid the conflict resolution and the work of healing, is the fertile space where new ideas and vision can find birth.*

A quick scan of published book and article titles focusing on pastoral transitions in congregational life describe these seasons as times of anxiety, trauma, and conflict, and of "being thrust into the fire." Some cast these liminal moments as "difficult" or "stormy," while one, somewhat more optimistically, called it a time of both "promise and peril." The most positive I found promised "refocusing and healing." But I believe we can do much better than this. I want you to come to believe that leadership transitions in the life of the local congregation can be exciting and transformative. Within the process of saying goodbye and letting go, amid the conflict resolution and the work of healing, is the fertile space where new ideas and vision can find birth. This can be a season in your life together with God that is full of creativity and possibility, one that is flush with the hope and promises of new life. While *transition* gives a name to change, *transformation* implies a dramatic remaking of who and what we are into a fuller reflection of who God envisions us to be. Pastoral transitions don't need to be negative experiences of loss and lack of direction; they can be seasons of celebration, healing, creativity, and experimentation individually and in the life of a congregation.

How do I know this is true? I have been a **settled pastor**, who has both arrived in a new placement and left an existing ministry setting. I have been an **interim pastor**, holding the settled pastor's place until she returned from sabbatical. I have been a **transitional pastor**,[1] leading others in a season of change, and I have been a congregant whose pastoral leader has left, wondering what in the world would come next. I have seen congregations whose transition became transformation, and some for whom it did not. This has led me to try to discover what makes such a change possible—what "best practices" inform this process and what it requires of the pastoral leader, of the congregation, and of God. As I researched and read, I noticed that there are many resources for clergy in transition, whether we are the leaders who are going or coming, those who hold the place, or those who keep things moving ahead in times of change. But there are few resources for individuals in local congregations who can or want to experience God's transformative power in the midst of leadership change. So this is for *you*!

The Announcement

Your pastor is leaving. You may have received the news in any number of ways. Perhaps you received a letter from your church moderator, president, council leader, elder, board chair, or from the pastor themselves. Maybe you had a phone call from someone who just couldn't keep the news quiet any longer. You might have heard this announcement from the pulpit on Sunday morning or at a midweek service. Regardless of *how* you heard, your interest in and need for this book has something to do with the fact that your pastor is leaving. They may be retiring, moving to a new congregation, or taking a job in an entirely different field, or they may have been asked to leave. In some circumstances, pastors leave because of ill health or even death. Any number of possibilities put you and your congregation in this place. This is where it all begins: the prelude to a new season in your church's life.

A *prelude* is "an introductory performance, action, or event preceding and preparing for the principal or a more important matter."[2] In worship, it is ideally the time when we begin to ready ourselves, physically, emotionally, and spiritually, for an encounter with the living God. This preparation is essential to our being fully present, fully engaged, and open to all that is possible in the moments, days, and weeks ahead. Thinking about the pastor's resignation as a prelude to what is to come allows us to frame the experience and all that follows as an act of worship, as an opportunity to engage the Spirit's full participation in the process of letting go, finding our way, and calling a new leader.

> *Thinking about the pastor's resignation as a prelude to what is to come allows us to frame the experience and all that follows as an act of worship.*

The news that the pastor is leaving can initiate an unsettling, challenging, and exciting season in the life of the church. **Change is difficult.** And pastoral change, whether the leader has been present for a decade or more, or for a much shorter time, has a profound impact on a local congregation. Often congregations don't know what to do next, where to turn for help, or what their options are. Many members have never lived through a pastoral leadership change, and those who have often are reluctant to take on the challenging work again. Each congregation will chart a slightly different course in getting from the "prelude" to the "benediction," the blessing of welcoming a new pastoral leader.

Some churches have the tradition that gives the outgoing leader the authority to choose the next pastor. In other churches, the choice of who to call is left entirely to the congregation. In some circumstances, temporary pastors are called to oversee the work of worship and pastoral care while the congregation begins its search; in others the denomination may have some say in what happens next and who is placed in leadership. There are many things to consider and many ways to move forward, so knowing your tradition, both locally and denominationally, is very helpful. No single process fits all churches. But there are things we can learn from all of these possibilities. Discovering the resources available from these experiences can inform and give shape to your congregation's next move.

Readying Ourselves to Begin

This book is a resource to help guide your transition experience. It is formatted with chapter titles that reflect a worship liturgy. Not every element is here, but I have chosen those that best direct our hearts and minds to the conscious expressions of worship that inform an intentional transformation process.

Chapter 1, "Call to Worship," defines the transitional tasks as the "work of the people." Entering into the season of transition in a worshipful manner frames all that is possible during this time. Personal and congregational self-examination are encouraged, and the choices you have for temporary leadership are defined and described. The first task is usually saying goodbye to the departing pastor, which is discussed in detail; how we end is as important as how we begin. We will talk about the mixed emotions of a pastor's departure and the importance of setting boundaries for healthy relationships past and present. All of these things are a part of where we begin as we hear a call to devotion to God and assume our work as God's faithful disciples.

Chapter 2, "Invocation," invites us to acknowledge our vulnerability and to seek both divine and human help during this transition process. Beginning with exploring some biblical figures who needed and asked for help, the chapter suggests people and places where congregations can find the help they need to navigate this season of change in seeking transformation. Awareness of our needs and where we can find support empowers us to live into transition with courage.

Chapter 3, "The 'Not Just for Kids' Conversation," takes a look at the importance of hearing not only the voices of our children and youth, but of all who are in any way related to our congregation, as we consider God's direction for both the present and the future. The five areas of ministerial concern identified in the previous chapter shape the kinds of conversations that are important during transition. Intentional, facilitated conversations that include all demographics involved in congregational life are added to by soliciting the input of those outside the congregation who can provide wider community perspective. Honesty about who the congregation is and what they hear God inviting them to is imperative for transformation.

Chapter 4, "Special Music," provides the opportunity to hear expressions and voices we don't normally experience in worship. Social and natural scientists William Bridges and Margaret Wheatley understand the inherent challenges and joys of organizational change and its relationship to us as human beings and participants in the natural world. Bridges views the work of transition in three overlapping stages: ending, the neutral zone, and beginning, while Wheatley examines patterns in nature that verify the reality that innovative change comes out of chaos. These voices inform our thinking about why we respond to change the way we do and what God might be up to as we seek transformation in our congregations.

Chapter 5, "The Word in Words," offers scriptural examples of both communities and leaders experiencing transition that leads to transformation. Citing a number of passages from the biblical text, I offer images that can be considered in preaching and Bible studies and in learning communities and other settings as congregations consider the qualities that make for successful leadership transition and God's invitation to transformation. Using God's story to inform and shape our own story deepens our investment in the work of change in biblical history as well as in our own lives.

Chapter 6, "Offering," suggests that more than money is needed to support transformative transition. The creation of safe space, the expansiveness of freedom, the discernment of new leadership, the compassion of understanding, and the discovery of new ministry all speak to what we can offer to one another and to God during a time of pastoral change. Cultivating our appreciation for all God has provided and for all we have available to return to God through the gifts we offer to one another results in tangible ways the congregation can serve one another and the wider community.

Chapter 7, "Communion," is an invitation to see our relationships in our congregations as sacrificial and redemptive during a time of change. Providing clear expectations by communicating honestly, negotiating healthy boundaries between departing and temporary pastors and the congregation, and navigating the challenges of social media during pastoral transitions factor into our ability to honor and respect each other and the season we've entered into. Such mutual accountability provides the best chance that everyone involved will be treated well and allowed the opportunity to deepen their sense of the ties that bind us to one another.

Chapter 8, "Hymn of Expectation," turns our attention to the end of the season of transition and the beginning of new pastoral ministry in a congregation. The work of transformation begun in this liminal time continues as preparations to say goodbye to the transitional leader and to welcome the new settled pastor exhibit some of what we have learned in the interim. A second goodbye is tempered with the excitement of a new pastoral relationship just ahead, and those engaged in a process that started with some degree of anxiety and trepidation anticipate resolution and peace.

Chapter 9, "Benediction," offers final words as the congregation moves from the season of transition into new ministry with the settled pastor. As a benediction sends people to do the work of God in the world, this chapter gives final affirmation for the tasks completed and blesses each with the hope and promise of fulfilling years of ministry to come.

Postlude: Appendices include supporting documents referenced in various chapters as well as some ways to incorporate ideas presented in the text into your congregational life.

Every chapter ends with a summation of the important Takeaways (key points) and with Congregational Resources you can use in your own worship, study groups, board meetings, and congregational gatherings. Traditionally, we consider the liturgy of the church to be the "work of the people." I want you to believe that *you* can lead transformation in your congregation during a pastoral transition.

I invite you to read with an open mind, to reflect with curiosity. Ask God's Spirit to take the words on these pages and expand them in your heart and imagination so that you and your church community may experience pastoral transition as transformation. Change is everywhere, but it need not be cause for dismay. Our dynamic, living God gives us the perfect example of what we can become when we are made anew!

Takeaways

- Change is inevitable, but it doesn't have to be negative.
- Framing a pastoral transition as a worship experience places us squarely in God's presence.
- Transformation implies a dramatic remaking of ourselves as well as of the congregation.
- We can experience God's transforming power in the midst of leadership change.

Congregational Resources

A Prayer in Response to Receiving a Pastoral Resignation

Holy One,
Remind us of your sustaining presence
as we hear and receive the news of our pastor's resignation.
A variety of feelings rise up within us;
walk with us in this new season in our congregational life.

We confess that we find change difficult,
and that we often experience transition as negative.
Enable us to see what lies before us as an opportunity to
deepen our dependence on you and to
discover your renewing and creative Spirit.

Bless our pastor.
Bless our congregation and the
community our church serves.
May we turn our heart's attention to your guiding presence for the coming days.
Let us not become anxious or afraid, but rather
seek the Spirit's wisdom as we celebrate what was and
look forward to what is yet to be.

Comfort us in this season of uncertainty and fuel our
hearts' hope in your future.
In the name of the One who lives among us,
Amen.

A Blessing for a Time of Transition

When change knocks on our door uninvited,
when we stand on the threshold uncertain whether to invite or hide,
when we are tempted to edit the past rather than engage
the future,
grant us courage, loving God, to welcome the unknown,
confident of our trust in You.

Notes

1. The term "settled pastor" refers to the pastor who is both called and installed by the congregation, or judicatory, to be the permanent spiritual leader of the congregation. An "interim pastor' is one who fills the pulpit and does limited pastoral care while a congregation is seeking a permanent leader. A "transitional pastor" or "intentional interim" is someone trained to lead congregations in reflection, assessment, conflict transformation and renewal while seeking new pastoral leadership.

2. *Merriam-Webster*, s.v. "prelude," accessed January 13, 2020, https://www.merriam-webster.com/dictionary/prelude.

CHAPTER ONE

CALL TO WORSHIP

We Are Called

Following the announcement that a pastor is leaving, things start to happen. There is much to think about and much to be done. Boards, committees, and individuals begin to spin out the implications, wondering what happens next; and jumping into the business at hand is tempting, even if we are not sure what that business should be! But *before* getting to all of that, I want to invite you to hear a call to our primary work, a call to worship.

The ancient Greek word *leitourgia* (λειτουργία) referred to a "ministry" or "sacred work" done by individuals as an offering to the gods in service of the people.[1] This term later became familiar to us in the word *liturgy*, the work of faithful people recognizing God, and in service to God and to one another. While we look to clergypersons to help shape, guide, and lead our liturgy, or the work of our worship of God, as followers of Jesus we each are called to worship God and serve both God and others; this is part of our faithful expression of discipleship.

"To call" is to initiate an action; it requires us to *do* something, either to offer the invitation or to respond to it. When we offer a "call to worship," we are inviting the gathered community to become acutely aware of the fact that our work, first of all, is to worship God. It is a summons to set aside all distractions so that we might enter into, if not physically, then spiritually, a sacred time and space where we honor and love God and, in doing so, expect God to be revealed. As we find ourselves thrust into a season of transition, this is an important place to start: by doing *our* work as God's own. Inviting one another into God's presence, knowing that in offering our worship to God, we can discover our strength and priorities for the future.

> *Intentionally inviting one another to be aware of and in tune with the Divine in our midst establishes a strong, faithful foundation for everything that lies ahead.*

While clergy often use the language of "call" to describe their own sense of purpose and motivation for life choices, congregants are also called to draw near to God, to imitate Christ, and to understand God's direction for their own lives and for their life together as the body of Christ. Beginning a season of transition by intentionally inviting one another to be aware of and in tune with the Divine in our midst establishes a strong, faithful foundation for everything that lies ahead. It demonstrates our dependence on God's leading, our commitment to Jesus' example, and our desire for the Spirit's infusion in the process of moving forward. By calling ourselves to a time of worship, focusing on what we can offer God, we have a secure base from which to launch ourselves into the work to come.

Called to Enter In

And what is the action that our call invites us to? The most immediate need is to be intentional about entering this season with thoughtfulness and grace. Many things seem pressing; a variety of emotions and responses cloud the atmosphere. Reminding oneself and others that not only is God with us, but that we are with God—that is, we are securely in God's providential care—helps put natural anxiety into a faith-filled context. We are not alone; others have traveled this path. God is with us; we are with God and God will be our guide.

Acknowledging that we are in God's presence in the midst of transition immediately begins to shift the focus: not to the departing pastor, not to the grieving (or otherwise) congregation, not to the uncertain future, but to our work as disciples to worship God, the One who will lead and provide. We are laying the groundwork for making a period of transition into a season of transformation when we foremost and repeatedly call ourselves to see this task as the work of the people in relationship to God. Part of that work is to address how we feel in the wake of the announcement of the pastor's leaving. Authentic worship demands that we bring our whole selves to God and expose our own truth. Honestly assessing where you are and how you feel about your pastor leaving is an important place to begin.

Called to Examine Our Feelings

As the news sinks in that the pastor is leaving, responses from the congregation will vary, depending on one's relationship with the pastor and the circumstances surrounding their departure. A pastor who is retiring after many years of faithful service will invoke an entirely different response than one whose exit comes after months, maybe years, of conflict, lethargy, abuse, or unrest. A pastor who resigns because of health concerns or dies unexpectedly leaves the congregation with yet another emotional response. Once you hear the news that the pastor is leaving and you begin to feel these emotions, you can be sure that your relationship with this pastor has already begun to change. Regardless of the particular circumstances, it is important to acknowledge that while each person's response is in some ways uniquely their own, there are commonalities in the reactions we experience when someone says goodbye.

Common feelings that arise when a congregation must say goodbye to a beloved pastor are grief and loss. We must be mindful that the grief expressed in this loss of relationship may be magnified by peoples' prior experience of grief and loss. William Bridges warns, "When old losses haven't been adequately dealt with, a sort of *transition deficit* is created—a readiness to grieve that needs only a new ending to set it off. . . . What they are actually reacting to is one or more losses in the past that have occurred without any acknowledgment or chance to grieve."[2] It may help to know that this is a usual occurrence in any loss but especially in the loss of a pastor. As a transitional pastor in one congregation, I continually heard the name of the former pastor, a beloved leader who had retired. It helped that this person was a friend of mine, and I appreciated the congregation's sense of loss. But it also brought up other losses of other pastors, some not so endeared to the congregation. Grief is compounded upon unprocessed grief.

If you have had a meaningful relationship with your pastor and view them as a confidant, spiritual supporter, leader, and friend, you might feel personally betrayed or saddened that this person has chosen to leave this relationship. It might feel personal, as if they were specifically leaving *you*. It helps to remember that pastoral leaders are called to serve the entire congregation, not select individuals within it. Your feelings of abandonment or loss reflect a meaningful relationship that is now in the process of change. You can honor that relationship by finding someone with whom to share your loss and grief, including, but not limited to, the departing pastor, so that you will have support when that pastor has gone. It might be appropriate to share your feelings in the context of a prayer group or Bible study and invite others to process this transition with you. You may want to speak to the pastor directly, acknowledging this change in your relationship and sharing your gratitude for what this person has meant to you. You may want to seek counseling or other professional support if you realize that this loss is bringing up earlier, seemingly unrelated grief.

Not everyone will feel the loss of a pastoral leader in the same way.

In the end, it is important to remember that ideally a pastor's leaving is a discernment of God's direction in their life and in the life of the church. Ultimately, it isn't about any one of us; it's about God. Attending to grief and loss are positive steps toward being ready to accept new leadership when that time comes.

Not everyone will feel the loss of a pastoral leader in the same way. If you have been less personally or positively engaged with the pastor, perhaps you feel more objective, sorry to see them go, but also eager to imagine a new leader. Your perspective can be helpful in framing the change for others, recognizing their discomfort while offering reminders of God's steadfast faithfulness.

If you have been involved with the pastor and view them negatively, perhaps because you or others in the congregation have experienced conflict, abuse, or neglect, you might be relieved that this moment has come and look forward to this departure. But you, too, have emotional work to do to set yourself on a course of healing and hope for the future. Congregations who have had a negative experience with a pastor are helped when a qualified leader does a congregational debrief after the pastor has gone. This process allows the opportunity to remember and celebrate the highlights of the pastor's tenure as well as to openly acknowledge the troublesome experiences. Together the congregation can decide what they have learned and want to carry forward, as well as what to leave behind as they begin to think about the future. (See appendix A, "A Congregational Debrief.")

> *Being intentional now will help establish a pathway for moving ahead; honesty with yourself and others is important in the work of transformation.*

And of course, one's response to a pastor leaving could be a combination of any number of feelings in addition to these, both positive—a sense of completion, that the time is right, genuine happiness for the pastor's next steps—as well as negative—anger, confusion, despair, apathy, fear, or even indifference. There is no one "right" way to feel, but it is important to consider how you feel and to think about how you want to acknowledge those feelings. Being intentional now will help establish a pathway for moving ahead; honesty with yourself and others inform our work of worship and is important for transformation.

Called to Intentional Goodbyes

If we hold that liturgy, or worship, is the work of the people, then we must be prepared to enter fully into our reverence for God in order to be effective. We cannot be distracted by other relationships that threaten to mix with or confuse our loyalty and devotion to God. Intentionally understanding how we feel, both individually and collectively, helps us to begin to accept the change we face and to say goodbye to our outgoing pastor. This will seem natural to some and strange to others. In some congregations, pastors come and go and return only by specific pastoral invitation for special occasions or celebrations. In others, pastors retire and remain a part of the congregation, sometimes are given emeriti/a status, and continue to be engaged in the daily concerns of ministry. Before reverting to whatever has been "normal" or "traditional" for your congregation, consider the impact of your former pastor's presence on the process of transition and new leadership before you decide what's best for your community.

A healthy transition, leading to the possibility of transformation, is supported by a clear, bounded relationship with the outgoing pastor. Saying goodbye is an opportunity to recognize the positive legacy a beloved leader leaves behind. A special celebratory occasion planned to reflect and express gratitude to the departing pastor makes everyone feel more positive about the transition, even if the congregation regrets the leader's decision. It also marks the end of a particular tenure of leadership, both freeing the outgoing leader from having any further responsibility for the congregation and liberating the congregation to choose new leadership. (A litany recognizing this new relationship is provided at the end of this chapter.)

In some cases, however, the parting is not so "sweet." If a pastor leaves on less than positive terms, it is still appropriate to mark this ending so that everyone recognizes that change is happening. If a celebration is inappropriate, invite members of the congregation to join the leadership and the departing pastor for a time of prayer, offering blessings for one another's ministries without judgment or accusation. (An example of this is found at the end of the chapter.)

> Overwhelmingly, most Protestant denominations agree that in the pastoral transition and early years of a new pastorate, the former pastor should have little to no contact with the congregation and its members.

In congregations where the pastor does not actually leave and intends to remain a part of the worshiping people, it is still wise to create boundaries that are supported by both the outgoing pastor and the continuing leadership to provide a separation of loyalties and make space for new leaders to come in. Have congregational leadership create these boundaries in conversation with the former pastor; the goal is to best serve the congregation during its season of change.

Outgoing pastors who intend to stay are wise to maintain a season of absence from the congregation as it discerns its next choices for leadership, perhaps even well into the first year of the new pastor's arrival. Failure to do this can result in a conflicted sense of loyalty among members and friends of the congregation, and reluctance to engage meaningfully with the temporary or settled pastoral leaders as they try to minister in this time of change. Daniel Hotchkiss, a senior Alban Institute consultant, suggests that individuals who are troubled about a pastor's departure consider these questions: "What part of my experience of the Holy depends on this representative of God who's leaving? What part of my anger and disappointment belong to the departing rector, and what part reflects my own unfinished business with my God?"[3]

While this season of separation may seem unfair or hurtful, a thoughtful outgoing pastor can build on their legacy of leadership by encouraging the congregation to seek God's new direction for their communal life and by supporting the new leaders as they begin. It is important to note here that overwhelmingly, most Protestant denominations agree that in the pastoral transition and early years of a new pastorate, the former pastor should have little to no contact with the congregation and its members. Some denominational clergy codes of ethics, such as the Transition Ministries ABCUSA Code of Ethics and The Covenant and Code of Ethics (appendix C), even require this separation.

This is an important consideration and conversation to have between the departing pastor and remaining congregational leaders. The decision to support this boundary is a commitment on the part of both to trust God and to realize that transformation happens only when we can let go of the past to embrace the future. Wise outgoing pastors who have genuine concern for their former congregation's growth and ability to thrive will honor and promote such boundaries.

Healthy goodbyes free both the departing pastor and the congregation to move in new directions. Tokens of appreciation, a celebratory reception or meal, and a special addition to worship that ritualizes the pastor's departure all help to create healthy closure. After the pastor is gone, congregants can continue to share and process their feelings together as a season of change becomes a season of transformation.

Called to Choose Transition

While there is clearly some degree of inevitability when it comes to change, you can actually choose what kind of transition your congregation will experience when your pastor resigns. Some congregations choose to minimize leadership transition and move quickly from one settled pastor to the next, often with the help of the departing pastor. This is most common when the retiring pastor identifies their successor or a pastoral "parent" grooms and promotes a literal or figurative "child" in the ministry. This may seem like an appealing shortcut to the transition process, but shortcuts don't eliminate the need for the work of self-examination, repair and restoration (if necessary), and envisioning that is part of a transformative process. Most congregations who do not invest the time, energy, and spirit into living in and through the work of transition in some way act out their unprocessed emotions and conflicts during the next pastor's tenure. They get to the final "answer" more quickly, but failing to afford themselves the opportunity to work through significant issues can later sabotage a new pastoral relationship. This results in change but not authentic transformation.

Much is written on the work that can happen in transition that may lead to transformation in congregations. Experts in transition ministry[4] agree on five general areas of focus for a congregation during this time. These include

- reflecting on a congregation's history,
- defining the makeup and values of the present congregation,

- understanding congregational patterns of leadership,
- evaluating and affirming relationships beyond the congregation, and
- thinking about the future. (See appendix B for explanations of each.)

Each of these areas can be addressed in a variety of creative, engaging ways to further invite God's Spirit into reflection and discernment. Without a season of transition, these areas don't usually get tended to, or do only after the new pastor arrives. The need to address these issues before doing anything else limits the new leader's ability to propose or engage anything new.

> *Dare to see the transition period as an opportunity for reflection, growth, and opportunity! Meaningful work leads to meaningful change.*

Choosing transition for your congregation affords the best opportunity to enter into this season with a clear intent to focus on God (the work of the people, remember?), to address one's feelings about the past, and to educate one another about what's possible in the future so the congregation can follow the Spirit's lead, not just in experiencing change but in *being transformed*. Dare to see the transition period as an opportunity for reflection, growth, and opportunity! Meaningful work leads to meaningful change.

Called to Know Our Need for Pastoral Leadership

In the context of being called to worship, doing the work of the people, we find safe space to examine our own needs. They will be different for each congregation. One congregation I served as transitional pastor needed to spend an entire year focusing on recovery from serious clergy mistrust and conflict; another congregation, after a long and healthy pastoral relationship, was able to focus on an entirely different agenda. Acknowledging what we need and asking for the time, leadership, and skills to address those needs contributes significantly to congregational health and transformation.

As you consider your congregational needs in light of your pastor's leaving, pastoral leadership for the season of transition should take priority over finding a permanent pastor. As you determine what you need, you can begin to think about who can fill that role and guide your congregation as you begin to make the transition to new leadership. Here there are many options; notice that some are more suited to initiate transformation than others.

SUPPLY PASTOR OR PULPIT SUPPLY, LICENSED MINISTER OR LAY MINISTER. These are individuals who can preach and lead worship on a week-to-week basis. They can provide flexibility and are best used for the short term, as in the weeks immediately after the outgoing pastor leaves and then again before the newly settled pastor begins. Supply pastors don't usually provide any other ministry services other than weekly worship; for example, they don't offer pastoral care or attend board or committee meetings. These leadership roles may be handled by existing lay leaders (e.g., deacons, church moderator) or by other staff pastors, associate ministers, or someone from the outside. This is a short-term solution. A member of the congregation who is a clergyperson or licensed lay preacher might seem like an obvious and easy choice for transitional leadership, but that person isn't likely to be entirely objective, specifically skilled, or able to provide an "outsider's look" at the congregation during this liminal time. Don't go with the easiest choice; seek the best choice! It really does matter.

INTERIM PASTOR. For the longer season of transition, you could consider an interim pastor. The word *interim* is associated with "filling a gap," such as the one left when your pastor departed. This person usually preaches weekly and attends to the basic pastoral needs of the congregation. They can be full- or part-time, and their responsibilities vary depending on the contract you agree on. They establish continuity and relationships, but they are generally not responsible for leading significant, transformative change. It is important to note that the interim pastor is not eligible to be a candidate for the pastoral position. (See appendix C, Transition Ministries ABCUSA Code of Ethics and The Covenant and Code of Ethics, and chapter 7, "Communion," for further discussion.)

TRANSITIONAL PASTOR OR INTENTIONAL INTERIM PASTOR. These are clergy who have training in leading change in congregations, in intentionally moving churches forward in ministry. These leaders engage the five movements named above as the work of this season, and many can also address patterns of conflict and grief. Healthy reflection, boundary-making, envisioning, and conflict transformation are usually among their skill sets. These leaders most often provide the best opportunity for turning transitions into transformational experiences.

> *Transitional pastors or intentional interim pastors most often provide the best opportunity for turning transitions into transformational experiences.*

MINISTERS AT LARGE. Some denominations enlist retired clergy to serve churches in transition on a temporary basis. Depending on their training and experience, these experienced clergy may fall into any one of the three categories named above. Your denomination would be able to help you secure one of these leaders, depending again on what areas you have identified as your need.

SUCCESSION LEADERSHIP. In this model derived from nonprofit organizations, the departing leader participates in and works with the incoming leader so that there is intentional overlap. This model can work in nonprofit organizations that value stability, promoting from within, and retention of organizational memory. However, "hiring from within may have advantages in not-for-profits, but it does not necessarily have them in congregations," reports pastor/teacher/community builder Donna Schaper. "If the previous pastor stays around, the parishioner has little chance for closure on an old relationship, thus all but prohibiting an in-depth relationship with the new pastor."[5] When succession leadership is envisioned in churches, this requires both the outgoing pastor and the incoming pastor to work together for several months at least, and for the church to pay both. This may look like what some congregations do when they promote internally, and it may be an entirely new idea for others. If this is your tradition or you want to try this model, proceed with caution and careful reflection. Significant opportunities for transformative work may be lost by not having a clear transition. It is important to think through how the work that is usually done in the transition time can happen in the midst of succession, when the end result, the next pastoral leader, is already decided. (Further discussion can be found in chapter 5, "The Word in Words.")

> *Knowing what your church needs in a transition leader is important if you intend this time to be transformative.*

Knowing what your church needs in a transition leader is important if you intend this time to be transformative. In some cases, it's pretty clear what a congregation needs when a pastor leaves; in others, it is less so. Start with asking the people in your congregation and community what they think they need, perhaps making use of survey instruments available from your denomination or judicatory. The condition under which a pastor leaves is the first clue as to what might be needed when they are gone. A long tenure of loving relationship may be followed by a great sense of loss or grief; a conflicted pastoral relationship often needs to be addressed by someone trained in conflict transformation. A sudden loss of pastoral leadership usually produces shock and perceived abandonment. By identifying your congregation's needs, you can begin to attend to them. There is no "one size fits all" here; without assessment, you will be taking a shot in the dark and may ultimately end up not addressing any of the actual needs.

Wise and intentional care of the church's needs at this time will position you to better serve the needs of those around you in the future. It is the work of the people to love and honor God; we do this best when we bring our true selves before our Maker.

Called to Know Our Need for Congregational Leadership

One of the first questions after the pastor resigns is usually, "Who is responsible to find leadership now?" Most congregations have a governing board or executive council, or a group responsible for nurturing the spiritual life of the congregation, particularly involving worship and pastoral care. Any of these groups could be the one that discerns the congregation's immediate needs and secures a suitable temporary pastor. This could be the same group that would work with this leader during the transition, freeing up the pastoral search committee to focus on finding the next permanent leader. The outgoing pastor may be able to suggest resources, but as a rule, they should not be the one to make decisions about who follows them, even temporarily. This is where the congregational leadership begins to take responsibility for choosing who and what happens next.

As the work of securing a temporary leader is underway, congregations may also begin considering who will lead the search for the next settled pastor. Your church bylaws or constitution should be the first place to look for direction on the makeup of this group. Generally, strong pastoral search committees are comprised of representatives of the congregation at large, with intentional inclusion of a variety of groups, including, but not limited to, gender, age, race or ethnicity, longevity in the congregation, sexual orientation, theology, education, and anything else your particular congregation values. The size of this group will depend on your membership, and it's important to remember that this group will have to serve for twelve to eighteen months in most cases, meeting regularly.

> *Having congregational affirmation from the start aids in building support for this group's work, trust, and authority, which will be important when they bring a candidate to be voted on later.*

It is best to have the congregation vote on the pastoral search committee members. Having congregational affirmation from the start aids in building support for this group's work, trust, and authority, which will be important when they bring a candidate to be voted on later. Ideally, those on the pastoral search committee would be temporarily released from other leadership responsibilities in the congregation during this season. This frees them to dedicate their time and energy to the search process, although this is not always possible in smaller congregations.

When should this vote take place? It could happen as early as the congregation can coordinate their efforts to make it possible, perhaps in the first three months after the outgoing pastor leaves. In cases where the pastor announces their departure many months in advance, the pastoral search committee could be established before the pastor actually leaves. In one congregation I served as transitional pastor, however, I did not recommend they choose a search committee until we had worked together a full year, debriefing and healing from the hurts of the previous pastor. Again, it will be different for each congregation. Remember that the immediate need is to secure a temporary pastor; with that person in place, you have time to constitute a search committee.

Called to Transformation

Although all these decisions seem daunting and are complicated by emotions surrounding the departing pastoral leader, this important work lays the foundation for a season of transformation. Remember, being called is an invitation to action, to be about the work of the people with intentionality and devotion to God. While there is much for us to do, it is all less important than what we invite God to do, which is why the "invocation" comes next.

Takeaways

- Being aware of and receptive to God's presence places our focus on God in our midst.
- Honest acknowledgment of our feelings allows us to attend to them in healthy ways, preparing us for new leadership.
- Boundary setting is important for moving into the future.
- The choices we make early in the transition process can set us up for transformation.

Congregational Resources

A Call to Worship in Times of Change

Come, worship the changeless God whose steadfastness is sure and whose mercy is everlasting!

Come, worship the ever-present God who makes a home
   among and within and between us!
Come, worship the wise and loving God who sees our needs,
   hears our cries, and knows what our hearts are feeling
   this day!
Come, worship and give thanks! God is in our midst!

A Call to Worship When Saying Goodbye

When the ties that bind us to one another begin to unravel,
when the cords that hold us loosen to set us free,
when the call that unites us moves us in different directions,
have mercy, O God, and gather us to yourself
that we might remember your love and compassion for us
   and prepare to live anew.

A RITUAL AND LITANY OF SEPARATION THAT CALLS US TO NEW LIFE

*On a table in the front of the worship space is a rhizomic
plant, perhaps an iris, lily, or bamboo. Alongside this
centerpiece are glass containers of unplanted bulbs,
visible to the congregation. They can serve as a focal
point as the outgoing pastor and a congregational leader
come to the front to share this litany. At the end, the
plant is given to the departing pastor as a remembrance
of the community in which their faith and leadership was
planted. The worshiping congregation is invited to take a
bulb and plant it outside or in a pot, reminding them of
the gifts they continue to nurture and grow to maturity as
an expression of God's beauty in the world.*

LEADER: A rhizome is a plant whose roots spread out
horizontally and send up shoots of new life in many directions, expanding and widening their reach as they mature
and grow. Iris, bamboo, and canna lilies are familiar
examples. The relationship between a pastor and a people

is also like this, widely connecting many individual shoots that bring life to the world. To remain healthy and productive, rhizomes, at regular times in their growth, need to be separated and given new space, uprooted and replanted, so they can continue to thrive and multiply.

When a pastor leaves, it is like the separating of rhizomes: the ground shifts, connections are exposed, we experience a sense of uprooting and replanting, discovering ourselves in new soil in which we can live and thrive. Old relationships are disturbed and change, but nothing is lost! In fact, it is in the separation that new life is possible, for both the plants and for us.

PASTOR: As I leave, I am aware of how grateful I am for the privilege of being your pastor. Together we have shared life and death, growth and fallowness, laughter and tears, struggle and joy. These experiences will always remain with me. While the roots of our relationship are grounded in our faith, I recognize that, like rhizomes, we must be separated and planted in new ground in order for each of us to reach the full potential of our growth.

PEOPLE: We have been encouraged by your spirit, inspired by your witness, comforted by your presence, challenged by your vision. Our lives have grown and matured together. Now as we come to part, we join you in this act of separation, freeing you to be planted in the new soil of your life, even as we are replanted in our own.

PASTOR: As I leave the pastorate of this congregation, I let go of the relationships that connected us in the community of worship and education. May God send you another to inspire, grow, and challenge your faith.

PEOPLE: As you leave us, we release you from the responsibilities of nurturing our faith and promise to continue to encourage growth in one another. As we move forward, we let go of the connection that assumes your pastoral care of us. May God honor your faithfulness and care for you as generously as you have cared for us.

PASTOR: I accept your release from the joys and concerns of pastoral care for this congregation and pledge to continue my prayerful support of you from a distance. I let go of that part of our relationship that required me to be called, needed, present, and included in your corporate and individual lives. May God fill those needs for us all by other means.

PEOPLE: We release you from serving us, and we let go of the expectation that you will be here for us. May God be present to us all in new and vital ways.

LEADER: It is never an easy thing to be uprooted, to say goodbye; it is a sign of God's blessing that we struggle to let one another go. But we trust in God's promise that we will be nurtured again in the fertile soil of a pastoral relationship as we seek a new leader to grow alongside us in faith.

PEOPLE: We are grateful for your ministry, and we trust God to guide us to new relationships and deeper faith. As you have blessed us, so we bless you with thanksgiving to our faithful God. We give you this [name of plant] as a reminder of how our lives were entwined; go with our love and gratitude for creating life and beauty with us.

PASTOR: Our life together comes to a close, but we will continue to be united in purpose as we bloom and grow, serving God in new ways. Come, each one, take a bulb. It is a symbol of your potential and your giftedness to the world. Plant it and yourselves in the soil of God's love, allowing the Spirit to nurture you all to life anew! (*People are invited to take a bulb with the help of ushers.*)

A RITUAL FOR A CONGREGATION AND PASTOR WHO IS DEPARTING AFTER CONFLICT

Pastors do not always leave congregations on good terms, but nonetheless, there is a need for closure for both the clergyperson and members of the congregation. If appropriate, congregational leaders may invite the pastor to the church at a time other than regularly scheduled worship and invite a particular board or group, or anyone who would like to participate, to join them. You may choose one or more persons to participate in leadership.

Be clear about what the ground rules are for this occasion as you invite people to participate. This is a ritual of departing and blessing, not a time of discussion or airing of grievances or complaints. Sit or stand in a circle. This way everyone can see one another and there is no "head," but all are viewed equally, even though there is leadership. You may want to have a single lighted candle, representing God's presence, on a table in the center of the circle; this will provide a focal point.

CONGREGATIONAL LEADER 1: We gather to say goodbye and to offer our blessing to one another in peace. We know that the path to this place has not been easy for anyone, and it is important that we treat one another with dignity and respect. We come not to discuss or debate but to pray and bless, releasing one another to seek healing and to continue to serve and love our God. We will offer a prayer for our departing pastor first and then for our congregation. We will conclude with a few moments of silence and then a blessing for us all. You are asked to leave quietly when we are done. Let us pray.

LEADER 1: Merciful God,
Thank you for accompanying us on life's journey,
    especially when the way is difficult.
Your presence with us gives us comfort and strength.

We gather to offer blessing and peace to [pastor's name] as we part company.

We are grateful for the ways in which [name] has blessed us and offered their gifts in our community.

Bless [name] with mercy and compassion as they look to you for direction and healing in the days and months to come.

Bless [name] with the gift of your grace that they might find a new sense of call and purpose in their lives as they continue to love and serve you.

Help [name] to forgive our shortcomings in this relationship and to be released from the temptation to harbor ill-will toward us.

Grant peace to [name] as they depart.

May the example of Jesus' loving-kindness and mercy be our guide. Amen.

Leader 2, already designated, prays for the congregation and community.

LEADER 2: Loving God,

We come in gratitude for your faithfulness.

Bless our congregation, represented by those who are gathered here.

Grant us strength of spirit and the compassion of kindness as we release [pastor's name] from our service.

Open our hearts and give us the courage to examine our own participation in all that has led to this moment.

Bless us as we journey on in faithfulness as your people.

Fill us with trust in your Spirit's guidance and hope for new ministry and leadership in the days ahead.

Help us to forgive [pastor's name]'s shortcomings in this relationship and release us from the temptation to harbor ill-will toward our departing pastor.

Grant peace to our congregation as we continue in your service.

May the example of Jesus' loving-kindness and mercy be our guide. Amen.

*Let there be a few moments of silence. Conclude with
Leader 1 offering this blessing to all:*

May the power of the Creator fill you with the promise
  and hope of life anew.
May the mercy of the Redeemer enable you to forgive
  yourself as you have been forgiven.
May the tender indwelling of the Spirit fill you with
  compassion and grace.
Go in God's peace to love and serve the world. Amen.

*Participants may be invited to greet one another and the
departing pastor silently or they may simply leave.*

Process for congregational debrief: see appendix A.
Description of the five areas of transitional ministry empha-
  sis: see appendix B.
Transition Ministries ABCUSA Code of Ethics and The
  Covenant and Code of Ethics: see appendix C.

Notes

1. Biblehub, s.v. "leitourgia," https://biblehub.com/greek/3009.htm.
2. William Bridges with Susan Bridges, *Managing Transitions: Making the Most of Change*, 4th ed. (Boston: Da Capo, 2016), 31.
3. Daniel Hotchkiss, "The Spiritual Challenge of Clergy Transition," *Congregations*, Summer 2004.
4. Loren Mead, *A Change of Pastors . . . and How It Affects Change in the Congregation* (Herndon, VA: Alban Institute, 2005), 18; Roger Nicholson, *Temporary Shepherds: A Congregational Handbook for Interim Ministry* (Herndon, VA: Alban Institute, 1998), 6–12; John Keydel, "Focus Points and the Work of the Congregation," in *Transition Ministry Today: Successful Strategies for Churches and Pastors*, ed. Norman B. Bendroth (Lanham, MD: Rowman & Littlefield), 2014, Kindle ed.
5. Donna Schaper, "Leadership Transitions: What the Nonprofit World Can Teach Us," *Congregations*, Winter 2009.

CHAPTER TWO

INVOCATION

Invoking God: A Prayer for Help

In a traditional worship service, the invocation usually follows the call to worship and opening singing. We have been called to the work of worshiping God. We have joined as community to express our desire to hear and respond to that call in song, and then we pray to "invoke" God; that is, we purposely ask for God's presence and help. In worship we are acknowledging that we cannot do or be everything God desires us to do and be on our own. We acknowledge that we are vulnerable. We need the support and filling of the Holy Spirit to move ever closer to becoming a true reflection of the body of Christ.

I lift up my eyes to the hills—from where will my help come?
—Psalm 121:1

When a congregation enters a season of transition, seeking God's help may seem to be a given. But it's important to be intentional. Few of us are comfortable with vulnerability, the very thing that opens us to accessing divine help. We are accustomed to thinking we can do things on our own, that cries for help expose weakness, that needing someone or something beyond ourselves reflects a lack of faithfulness in our own God-given capacity. In fact, the opposite is true. Popular sociologist Dr. Brené Brown talks a lot about vulnerability. She writes, "Vulnerability is not winning or losing. It's having the courage to show up when you can't control the outcome."[1] When we "show up" to God, when we worship in the season of transition and change, when we can't control what is happening around us, we are in fact courageously placing our trust in the One who loves us faithfully. What a life-giving place to be!

We seek God's encouragement as we face uncertainty. We seek God's comfort as we experience loss and grief. We seek God's wisdom as we discern next steps. We seek God's imagination as we dare to consider change. We seek God's vision as we move toward transformation. We dare not take any of these for granted! Remember, change happens, but it isn't always transformational. Rearranging the furniture doesn't create a new room. Swapping leaders doesn't guarantee a new way of being in relationship. If we seek to be transformed, we must first become vulnerable, then seek God; we must invite God's help as we become the congregation and ministers God envisions us to be.

Throughout the biblical text, God's presence is invoked to affect the lives of the faithful in critically vulnerable times. The Psalms are full of invocations as repeatedly the *faithful* call out to God, asking for help. "I call upon the LORD, who is worthy to be praised, so I shall be saved from my enemies" (Psalm 18:3) is one example. Psalm 121:1-2 is another: "I lift up my eyes to the hills—from where will my help come? My help comes from the LORD, who made heaven and earth." Moses asked for what he needed to fulfill God's call in Exodus 4:10; Samuel called on God to send thunder and rain in 1 Samuel 12:17-18. The woman described in the synoptic Gospels as one who was bleeding asked for Jesus' help when she reached out to touch him in Mark 5:27-29. Even the apostle Paul invoked God's assistance as he struggled to keep the faith (2 Corinthians 12:8-9). Expressing their vulnerability, they all opened themselves to divine transformation. The congregation in transition is in good company when they invoke God's help during this season of change. No matter how organized, competent, and faithful we are, we cannot live into our potential without God's help.

An expression of our faithfulness is acknowledging that we are dependent on God for everything.

From Where Will Our Help Come?

During the transition that begins once your pastor has resigned, you *will* need help. Let's begin by affirming that we all need God's help all the time! An expression of our faithfulness is acknowledging that we are dependent on God for everything. Certainly God helps us in myriad ways: through direct action and response, through the love and grace of another, through our community and the wider world, through those with experience and expertise in the situations in which we find ourselves. Just as you would call a plumber if your sink was leaking, congregations need to access the resources that are available to them during the time of transition. When we ignore them and think we can do it on our own, we might find ourselves neglecting the gifts of God's help that have been provided for us.

Our Help Comes from People Who Pray

Perhaps the most empowering way a congregation can seek God's help is to commit to pray together regularly during the transition from one pastor to another. You may already have a prayer group; they can become the leaders for this effort. If you do not, perhaps now is a great time to begin one. Praying with a common purpose is a powerful way to unite people of all ages and abilities. Everyone can pray!

You may want to begin this effort by having a gathering to excite people, enlisting them to commit to praying for God's direction and guidance, inspiration and vision. This can be done in person or virtually. Explain your idea to bring the congregation together with this shared action; outline a plan for how and when to pray, and what to pray for. Invite people to sign up for various opportunities: a weekly prayer group, a once-a-month prayer vigil, a prayer partner, an online prayer community. The possibilities are wide ranging and can suit individual and congregational needs. Make sure to enlist children and youth as well; what a wonderful opportunity for all to learn about and increase their prayer life as together you invoke God's help.

Our Help Comes from the Departing Pastor

One of the responses to asking for God's help might come from the pastor who is leaving. How much help the departing pastor can be to the ongoing work of the congregation may be related to how the church feels about this person and their leaving. If the relationship between the congregation and pastor has been strong and generally positive, this person can do much to start the transition off on the right foot. If the relationship between the pastor and the congregation has been strained or compromised, then the ability of the departing pastor to help the congregation move forward may be more limited. Assess your sense of the relationship between the leader who is leaving and those who remain. This will begin to inform how much help you might receive from the departing pastor.

> *Assess your sense of the relationship between the leader who is leaving and those who remain.*

Let's assume you have had a healthy, positive relationship with your pastor who is now leaving. You can invite that person to help the congregation initiate the transition process in a number of ways. A spiritual leader or the group responsible for the spiritual life of the congregation might meet with the pastor to hear general pastoral concerns. Although the departing pastoral leader should never violate confidentiality with anyone, they can alert those who will be responsible for pastoral care to the needs of people in the congregation in a general way; for example, those who have experienced death and loss will need support as they continue grieving. Those hospitalized or in care facilities will need to be visited. Your departing pastor can prepare and even train people to take on these tasks at least temporarily. It would be a gift to the congregation and its leadership if they did.

Another way your departing pastor can be a vehicle of divine help is to initiate intentional closure with individuals and the congregation as a whole. As the pastor preaches, teaches, and works with groups and one-on-one with people to understand and transition to the future without their leadership, they are preparing the way for all that is to come. Clear establishment of their boundaries with the congregation both during the transition and afterward is definitely a part of this education. Have your leadership meet with the pastor to create boundaries and a plan to share them repeatedly with the congregation. God's help is evident in the pastor who loves their congregation enough to part with them well.

Our Help Comes from the Denomination

God's help can come from your denominational relationships. Most denominations have resources to help congregations during the time between settled pastors. What is available to you may vary according to your region or judicatory, but help is out there. The resources range the gamut from people to print and digital material, all in an effort to understand congregational needs and to offer best practices for what to do in a variety of situations. The best resource might be your closest denominational leader. A call to their office or an email alerting them of your congregation's leadership change can set the ball in motion. In some traditions, the path is quite well defined; in others, the direction you take will be your choice among several possibilities. Talk to denominational leaders and other churches you may know who have been in transition and used the resources you are considering; their learning can be of help to you.

American Baptists, for example, choose their own pastoral leaders, including their temporary (transitional or interim) leaders. Names and biographical information of these people can be acquired from your regional or national offices. Some regions have guidelines for how to proceed (e.g., "Equipped to Serve Anew: Guidelines for Pastoral Transition in the Philadelphia Baptist Association") and others will share anecdotal evidence to direct your way. Those who know something about your congregation may be in the best position to direct your next steps, because they may be aware of the issues and potential pitfalls of your particular community. But don't assume; check out all the resources you can get your hands on. More information is better than less!

In addition to local denominational offices, national denominational organizations also have helps (and usually websites). Many provide a database of pastors trained in transition ministry or who are available for temporary leadership. Don't think you are limited by geography; programs such as Ministers-at-Large move experienced clergy across the nation to respond to temporary pastoral calls for transition leadership.

Our Help Comes from Those Who Have Gone This Way Before

You may find God's help within your congregation. Depending on how long ago your congregation had a pastoral transition and pastoral search, you might have people in your community who were a part of securing the departing pastor (or an earlier one), and they might be able to inform the current process from this unique perspective. Of course, your congregation isn't likely to be the same or need the same things as it did the last time it experienced this kind of transition, but knowing something about your church's personal history of the change in pastoral leaders can be helpful.

For example, if the last time there was a pastoral search process, things went off the rails because the search committee failed to involve the congregation, knowing that could help you to ensure that it doesn't happen again. Likewise, if the last process went particularly well, or a helpful resource was identified then, it would be encouraging to know about it now. Another source for past experiences is your church archives or history. But recognize that often what we put in writing for record keeping doesn't tell the whole story; it's better to check in with those who were a part of the process if possible.

Being acquainted with the best practices of interim or transitional leaders will empower you to make good choices when deciding who should lead your congregation during this time.

Other reliable sources for help are the numerous written resources available in print or digital formats. As I said at the outset of this book, many of the resources available about congregational transitions are written with the temporary leader in mind; few are like this one, written for congregants themselves. But that doesn't mean you shouldn't use them. Being acquainted with the best practices of interim or transitional leaders will empower you to make good choices when deciding who should lead your congregation during this time. You can know what skills and emphases are important to lead you in the direction your congregation seeks to go. While you don't have to become an expert, it is relatively easy to become informed. The more you know about the help that is available, the better able you will be to tailor it to your congregation's particular needs.

Our Help Comes from Within

Strangely enough, sometimes the resources we need are close at hand, but we fail to recognize or use them. Consider that what your congregation may need in terms of encouragement, professional expertise, and giftedness might already exist in your congregation. Do you have a therapist or counselor in your church? Perhaps that person can share ideas about how to support people in crisis or experiencing grief. Do you have an educator in your congregation? That person might be able to organize some learning events as the congregation figures out their denominational process for transition and shares that with the wider group. Do you have people gifted in leadership, organization, hospitality, cooking, or skills like carpentry or home repair? How can they be called on to share their gifts during this transition period? You might utilize them for everything from organizing committees to preparing congregational meals and celebrations, to renovating the pastor's office for a new leader, to considering new outreach into the wider community! The transition season is a time to invite *all* to share their gifts and for the congregation to recognize that God has placed within them a wide variety of people and talents to be used in loving service. This may be the opportunity to view one another as an answer to the communal call for God's help; God's provision may already be in your midst!

> *The transition season is a time to invite all to share their gifts and for the congregation to recognize that God has placed within them a wide variety of people and talents to be used in loving service.*

Be assured that as we turn to God for help, God is already gifting each community for the needs within it. God's help will come to you during this season of transition from many places, both within and outside your congregation. Don't go it alone; look for and use the resources that are available to you, viewing each as God's gift for furthering your ministry and God's reign among us. Doing so is an affirmation of one another, an affirmation of community and of God's abundant mercy and grace.

Takeaways

- Be intentional about asking God for help, noticing that God's help often comes by way of others.
- Recognizing our own vulnerability opens us to God.
- Regular prayer is an important part of seeking God.
- A variety of resources are available in your congregation and from your denomination that can inform and support both your pastoral search and your time of transition.

Congregational Resources

A Prayer of Invocation

Holy God, we confess that we have convinced ourselves that by gifting us with many blessings, you have released us from our need for you. Forgive our arrogance, we pray, and hear our prayer for help. Guide us as we seek new direction and leadership during this unfamiliar season in our lives together. Keep our hearts and minds open to the people and ideas you will send to us that we might seek you in each and find you in all. Give us the courage to be vulnerable and, in so doing, see those who come alongside us as your gifts to us. Grant us the wisdom of your Holy Spirit and the tender heart of your Son, Jesus, in whose name we pray. Amen.

Guidance for a Praying Congregation

If you already have a prayer group or prayer partners in your congregation, you are well on your way to invoking God's help. During this season you might invite these groups/individuals to consider the congregation and its needs and concerns as a priority amid other prayer requests.

STARTING A PRAYER MINISTRY. There are any number of ways to begin a prayer ministry in your congregation, both formally and informally. If you want to keep it informal, you might ask a few people to regularly place before the congregation, either in person or electronically, the concerns of the transition process and the pastoral search so that people continue to be aware of the need to pray for these efforts.

If you chose to use this time to create a more formal/directed/organized process, you might consider the following:

- Initiate the effort to begin an intentional prayer focus with a gathering of some sort: an after-worship luncheon or reception, a special meal, a sermon series or special worship service, a called meeting of the church, an online group chat or group session. Any of these can be used as a launch platform to begin your prayer ministry.
- Explain the need: read passages of scripture that invoke God's help and tell Bible stories and share personal testimonies of those who asked for God's help and received it. Keeping these examples in mind can be encouraging.
- List some specific things that your congregation needs to pray for: pastoral and lay leadership, resources, vision, hope, healing, assurance, and so on.

- Decide how you will organize: partners, triads, small groups, existing groups, phone groups, online groups, large events, or a variety of these as best suits your congregation. Don't leave out people who physically can't attend due to age, ability, health, or distance: this is one ministry nearly everyone can be involved in! Seek to engage the most diverse, inclusive community possible.
- Whatever way you decide to "gather," have people make connections at your event. Ask them to share contact information and set their first few meeting times and dates, making sure everyone understands their next steps.

KIDS CAN PRAY! We are never too young to learn to pray. Encourage your children to invoke God's presence, help, and blessing in their lives and for the wider good. You can do this by teaching and modeling prayer in your learning-community activities. Consider these ideas as well:

- **Arrange kids' prayer partners** by encouraging them to share their prayer requests each week and then having each child commit to praying for another child for a week. When you gather them again, have the pairs talk together about what they did, how they prayed, and what happened for each. Share new requests and repeat or change partners and start again. This is a wonderful opportunity to teach children not only to voice their need but to take on the concern of one other person for a week and consider how God uses each in the lives of the other.
- **Create a prayer visual** by cutting out leaves and making a prayer plant on a wall, low enough for children to have access to it. Have them add their prayers on "leaves" (the youngest ones will need adult help), and then gather them to pray from those prayers when you are together. Another idea is to have them take a leaf with them, pray that prayer for the week, and return it the next week for another.
- **Grow "prayer plants"** (*Maranta leuconeura*). Have kids plant and grow prayer plants, or purchase small ones for each child. These plants are called "prayer plants"

because they literally lift their leaves, as if in prayer, each evening. (You can show kids a time-elapsed video of it here: https://www.youtube.com/watch?v=cRToxjXhbso) Ask children to care for their plants and, as they do, pray for one another, their church, and the world.

- **Create a prayer ritual.** Create a prayer ritual for children/ youth to learn and practice. Invite them to find a quiet place in their home where they can be quiet/alone. Ask them to gather a few items that are precious to them or that speak to them of God's love and care (i.e., something they picked up in nature, a favorite toy, a picture, a book). Ask them to sit quietly in that space three times every week for three minutes (keeping it short, simple, easy to remember). Ask them to breathe deeply from their bellies (practice this together) three times, paying attention to their breath. Follow this by a simple fill-in-the-blank prayer: "Thank you God for . . ."; "Please help [someone else's name] . . ."; "Please help me. . . ." End with another three belly breaths and "Amen." (Do this when you have kids together so they will learn the pattern, expanding the time and the prayer lines as they get older and more comfortable.) Talk about how they can use this prayer space they created to calm themselves when anxious or angry, to comfort them when hurt or sad, to celebrate when joyful or happy. Your check-in with them can be in person or online.

Exploring Vulnerability

These questions could be used as a personal reflection for congregants of any age as part of a Bible study or at the beginning of a leadership meeting.

1. Describe a time when you felt vulnerable. What was that like? Name the feelings that were connected to this experience.
2. What were you taught by your family, your educational setting, your society/culture about vulnerability?

3. Review the scriptures noted in this chapter as examples of faithful people who invoked God's help. What characteristics do you think they have in common? What happened as a result of their prayer?
4. Name other individuals or circumstances in scripture where God is called upon to help. What do we do with the tricky ones, like the ones who call on God to kill our enemies? How might we understand those?
5. What need do you and your church have right now? How might you invoke God's presence to address this need? What do you hope might result?
6. Wrap up your discussion by invoking God's help in a particular situation in which you feel vulnerable today. Trust that God will hear your prayer and respond.

Note

1. Brené Brown, *Dare to Lead: Brave Work. Tough Conversations. Whole Hearts* (New York: Random House, 2018), 19–20.

CHAPTER THREE

THE "NOT JUST FOR KIDS" CONVERSATION

Not Just a "Children's Sermon"

Many worship services that include children dedicate time to focus the message of the day for kids; as a pastor, I have always made it a priority to welcome and include children and youth in worship. While some congregations refer to this as the "children's sermon" or "children's moment," I refer to this as the "kids' conversation" and treat it as such, a conversation. I don't talk *at* them; I talk *with* them. I ask open-ended questions, welcoming their unscripted responses. It's risky; it sometimes doesn't go the way I predicted. It forces me to listen carefully and to be genuine in return. And it is frequently these conversations that become the most meaningful moments in the entire service as young voices ask honest questions and speak God's deepest truth.

> *. . . these conversations that become the most meaningful moments in the entire service as young voices ask honest questions and speak God's deepest truth.*

When we boil down what we have to say so that the youngest among us can understand, then it seems that most everyone else can too. This time in worship can be creative, playful, engaging, hands-on, soulful, honest, vulnerable, and direct—a wonderful opportunity for speaking truth about the challenges and opportunities of a season of transition that leads to transformation. I recall a particularly poignant Sunday immediately following the bombing of the Murrah Federal Building in Oklahoma City when I was responsible for the kids' conversation. Nineteen children had died. I don't remember the specifics of what I said, but I was truthful, shared my profound sadness, and allowed the children to express their feelings of confusion and grief as well. Together we searched for God's presence. I have no recollection of the "real" sermon that day, but many adults spoke to me about how meaningful the kids' conversation was as they processed their own anguish and disbelief. These times in worship with our children offer more than entertainment for adults; they recognize each voice, legitimize our experiences, and reveal the strength we can find together.

Jesus' welcoming of *all* people reminds us that in the time of transition, it is important to be sure that everyone is included in the conversation. Our love and respect for children and youth can be demonstrated when we include them in appropriate ways in our communal life. This is the kind of experience you can have as you invite people to share with one another and live into intentional, transformative transition. "Courageous conversations" some call them. They are an important place for transformation to begin.

Let's Start a Conversation

Pastoral transition opens up space for honest conversation; in fact, for this season to become transformative, this element of open communication is essential. Experiences with the previous pastor, both positive and negative, need to be retold. Assumptions about the congregation, its leadership, and its future need to be exposed. Questions need to be answered. Possibilities need to be explored. And vision and hope need to be cultivated and shared as ministry is reimagined and the congregation moves forward. These kinds of conversations—held intentionally, among the most people possible, representing the diverse makeup of the congregation, with clear, present, and informed leadership—can set the stage for charting a new course or for reviving a familiar one as the congregation discerns God's call to their particular ministry in this particular time and place.

> *Informal communications do not replace the need for scheduled, thoughtful, facilitated conversations that include as many people as possible from as many groups as possible.*

During the transition, inevitably much conversation *does* happen. But often it's held off the record—over the pews on Sunday morning, around the coffee pot in the kitchen after Bible study, in the nursery when parents drop off and pick up children, through email or text, even in the barber shop and grocery store in the community. "Official" conversations may happen as well, although they will typically reflect the thoughts and ideas of those who are heard with regularity. All the same, it can seem like everyone is talking! But in reality, many people are left unheard. Informal communications do not replace the need for scheduled, thoughtful, facilitated conversations that include as many people as possible from as many groups as possible. Every voice needs to have the opportunity to be heard as, collectively, you seek new direction for your life together.

There's Much to Talk About

Recall that the Call to Worship chapter identified five areas of exploration for a transition season (detailed explanations are found in appendix B). Again, they are

- reflecting on a congregation's history,
- defining the makeup and values of the present congregation,
- understanding congregational patterns of leadership,
- evaluating and affirming relationships beyond the congregation, and
- thinking about the future.

These topics need not be addressed in any particular order; in fact, they often **arise** organically and weave in and around one

another across the timespan a congregation has with an intentional temporary pastor. We will consider each of these topics
in the next few pages as we think about the issues they raise.
But there is also no need to limit yourselves to just these topics
for conversation. God's future for the life of your congregation is
awaiting discovery, and you can discern it together.

> *Looking backward is useful for most congregations because retrospect*
> *offers a sense of trajectory and purpose across time.*

Conversations about the Past

Looking back is a starting point for churches in transition, in part
because it is in some way easiest. After all, we know where we
have been—even if we don't entirely agree on what brought us
to our current position or on what might lead us forward from
here. Looking backward is useful for most congregations because
retrospect offers a sense of trajectory and purpose across time.
Looking back is particularly critical for churches whose departing
pastors caused pain or injury during their tenure. In chapter 1,
"Call to Worship," a debriefing process was suggested as a process to facilitate healing. (See appendix A.) Debriefing is one way
to organize our thoughts about the past. Another like it is to draw
on the wisdom of the African Sankofa tradition, characterized by
the saying, "It is not taboo to go back and retrieve what you have
forgotten or lost." This Akan tradition has also been described as
a way to "pick up the gems of the past. [It is a] constant reminder
that the past is not all shameful and that the future may profitably
be built on aspects of the past."[1] But it isn't only congregations
with conflicted pastoral histories that benefit from looking back
at previous leadership relationships and reconnecting with what
you discover there. Every congregation should pause at particular points in the journey to take stock of where they have been,
name what they have learned, notice how they have changed, and
gather the wisdom of the past to bring forward into the future.

Call it a "debrief" or the "wisdom of Sankofa," or pair it
with an anniversary, and you can create a delightful, informa-
tive, inclusive conversation that will help position you for further

conversations about what lies ahead. By including everyone in this process, the longevity of some can inform those who are considered newcomers, while the fresh look of those who are not emotionally invested in the past can illuminate those who are. Everyone participates and everyone learns! The results are a deeper understanding of what has taken place and how it has affected individuals and the system as whole. The conversation will also begin to identify the experiences, examples, shared traits, and values that are important for understanding the present congregation and for envisioning service to God in the years ahead. (Ideas for how to do this are at the end of the chapter.)

> *The transition time is a great opportunity to get in touch with both our assumptions and our realities.*

Conversations about the Present

Who and what we actually are and how we perceive ourselves are often very different from one another. The transition time is a great opportunity to get in touch with both our assumptions and our realities. Creating or completing an updated profile of your congregation is a helpful way to do this. Information regarding membership (active, inactive, and other categories), attendance, age and gender distribution, race and ethnicity, economic and educational levels, and updated contact information are all helpful in composing an accurate picture of who your congregation is today.

In one congregation where I was the transitional pastor, they insisted on having a Good Friday breakfast at 6:00 a.m. Living forty-five minutes away meant an early wake-up call for me, after being present for and driving home from the Maundy Thursday service the night before. I also needed to preach at the Good Friday service that evening. But I complied; I arrived at 5:45 a.m. for a lovely breakfast. As we sat eating, I asked those at my table to tell me the story of how this event got started and why so early in the day. It seems that the food had always been prepared and served by the men who had to go to work. So they came to cook and eat early, leaving the cleanup to those few who were retired.

I looked around at those seated; not a single one of them was still employed. All had retired years ago. They were awkwardly surprised when I pointed that out. And the next year they moved breakfast to 8:00 a.m.! They had been operating out of the perception that they were who they *had been* years before; they needed to see themselves as they were today in order to adjust their expectations for the present and the future.

As you assess your current reality, you may include other categories of data, such as occupations, percentage of students or retired persons, maps locating members' residences, church group identification and attendance, as well as current budget, staffing, and property assessment. The more information you can gather about your current situation the more resources you have to consider how best to utilize those as you move into the future. In addition, compiling as complete a portfolio as possible of your current reality will help you to assess some dimensions of your present health and provide the most accurate information for potential pastoral candidates. Besides, it can be fun! Involve as many people as possible and turn this fact-finding hunt into another opportunity for discerning conversation about yourselves and what these things say about your life together with God.

> . . . *ask people to think about and share what is not negotiable with them—in other words, to ask, "What would you not compromise in terms of your values and faith?"*

But demographics and other statistics don't tell the whole story of who we are. It's important to start a conversation about congregational values, about what's important to the congregation and how the members understand themselves. This will help discern what kind of leadership will be needed going forward. Create opportunities where congregational members can talk in groups about where and when they experience God, about their heartfelt understanding about what it means to be the church, and about what they value most in a community of faith. This could be the time to ask people to think about and share what is not negotiable with them—in other words, to ask, "What would you not compromise in terms of your values and faith?"

To do this you must create a space that is safe and conversation that is respectful and open. If you can establish those criteria first, responses to these inquiries can reveal even more of what is at the heart of individuals in your congregation. If you can't reasonably expect that such a conversation can be had without creating difficulty between people, then pass on this one. There are other ways to call out your congregation's values and "essentials" without alienating anyone. (See Congregational Resources below for practical suggestions.)

Conversations about Leadership

Congregational leadership takes on added importance in the midst of pastoral change. By this I mean not only the paid staff in addition to the pastor and the volunteers who serve on boards and committees but also those who are involved in other ways. In churches where the leadership is active and respected, elected openly and regularly, following a process that is endorsed by the congregation, individuals often find themselves doing more of the day-to-day work of ministry when the church is in transition. New seasons call for new responsibilities, some that may become permanent and others that are only temporary.

Using the transition as an opportunity to review leadership needs and resources and to explore new styles of leadership and new models of organizational structure is helpful. How does leadership function as part of your larger congregational system? Does what you are currently doing make the best use of your resources for the ministry to come? What are the qualifications for various leadership positions, and who might become leaders when asked for this special season, providing them an opportunity to step up and offer their gifts? Don't ignore the informal "leaders" in your congregation who may not have a title but who carry the kind of social capital or influence that should not be ignored. How are these people enlisted in the effort to transform your community?

> *Since change is inherent in a pastoral transition, embrace the opportunity to explore together.*

While experimenting with the mechanism of leadership may add to the disruption of this time, it may also provide some freedom for shifting responsibilities as you consider what works best. Freeing up existing leaders to serve on the pastoral search committee, for example, could provide the opportunity for new leaders to take a turn in positions previously limited to those who have been involved for many years. Changing or sharing duties might help individuals discover new gifts and the congregation find new resources that have been untapped until now. Since change is inherent in a pastoral transition, embrace the opportunity to explore together. God may be showing you a new way to work together to serve one another and the wider world. (See ideas for how to do this at the end of the chapter.)

Conversations about Our Relationships beyond Ourselves

Healthy conversation nurtures strong relationships within our congregations; the same can be true for our relationships outside our congregations as well. Creating an updated profile of your church in this area of identity will also be clarifying. What groups does your congregation belong to? Are you related to a denomination and, through it, a local region or judicatory? Do you partner with a food bank in the community, a homeless shelter, or a thrift shop? Do you give money to local service organizations, national or international missions, or other groups? Who or what in the community around your church do you have a relationship with? Local businesses, schools, or nonprofits? Other faith communities, whether ecumenical or interfaith? Residential neighbors?

A pastoral transition is a wonderful season in which to check the health of these relationships. Reach out to those individuals and organizations with whom you have been connected to see how they are experiencing your involvement in their work and to discern whether this is a relationship the church needs and wants to continue investing in for the future. Just because the previous pastor was a member of a particular organization and represented the church doesn't mean that the congregation is obligated to continue that relationship if it no longer resonates with the community of faith.

I recommend following Jesus' strategy: send out two people to interview these groups to update your information about them and to bring back impressions for further congregational review and discernment. You might want to send people who have no previous experience with this organization so that they can get a fresh look while assessing the relationship your organization shares. In addition, send pairs in which at least one person is comfortable in having this conversation; the second person can gain confidence from them. Finally, send pairs that represent different congregational demographics; that way each may be looking and listening for different things, increasing your ability to assess the relationship.

In doing this you will continue to be intentional about how you use your time and resources, with the possibility of strengthening relationships outside the congregation that matter to your ministry and letting go of those that don't align with the church's passions, freeing up space for new connections to form and grow. (See Congregational Resources below for ideas.)

> . . . *exploring new ministries during the transition time is a way of discerning God's invitation for the future.*

Conversations about the Future

Some congregations don't want to talk about the future during a pastoral transition; they choose to wait until the new pastor arrives to begin the process of envisioning. While there is some merit to that thought, exploring new ministries during the transition time is a way of discerning God's invitation for the future. It is also an opportunity to stop doing things that no longer have meaning.

Routines can be a gift and a hindrance. We don't generally question whether to brush our teeth each day; we just go ahead and do it, creating a healthy routine that serves us well. In a similar way, programs often become routine in churches, but not always to their credit. Periodically assessing the health of groups and organizations within the church, to consider their contribution to the life of their participants and the wider communion, and to celebrate their ending when their positive contributions have seemingly reached an end, is appropriate and wise. Ministries that no longer meet present needs can be transformed into new outreach. Groups whose effectiveness has all but burned out can be rekindled or extinguished, freeing space, time, and energy for creating something new.

Without such assessments, groups and ministries can become fossilized, hard to remove, taking up physical, emotional, and mental resources that could be directed toward something more vital and relevant. The transition season in the life of a congregation is a great time for experimentation. We learn by doing! Invite experiments with new ministries, perhaps on a trial or short-term basis; review them at an agreed upon interval and discover whether you are hearing a call to something new. If, in fact, you are discerning a new call, you might have a clearer understanding of the kind of pastoral leadership you will need to continue this important work.

Let's Talk: The Conversation with Kids

As I said at the beginning of this chapter, transformative conversations are intentional and inclusive; every group, individual, and organization within the congregation should be involved. Children and youth are no exception. Often they get left out of important events in the life of a worshiping community because it's assumed that they are too young to care or understand. Children, however, are an important part of a congregation.

> By modeling honesty and compassion, you are teaching young children that change is a part of loving and growing.

Our youngest children may not understand what it means to experience a pastoral transition, but they are likely to pick up on the emotional energy that surrounds them when they sit in worship or play in the nursery. Kids are great sponges, soaking in the dis-ease and sadness, joy and gratitude that swirl around them. Invite them in by talking about what's happening in terms they can understand. Include them in the pastoral goodbye by participating in an age-appropriate celebration or activity. Talk to them about saying goodbye and hello; make them aware of changes and help them, even at an early age, to appreciate the joys and challenges that change brings. Reassure them that the adults who care for them in worship and in their learning community will continue to watch over them, love them, and care for them. By modeling honesty and compassion, you are teaching young children that change is a part of loving and growing. It's on these foundational experiences that we build our responses to change later in life.

For children in elementary or middle school, the departure of the pastor may be a strange and painful thing. It's not likely that they anticipated that this person would ever come or go; most often children assume the pastor is just "there," like everyone else. These children may have formed a relationship with the pastor; the pastor may have baptized or christened them, taught them, related to them during a special time in worship designed for them, or played with them. You will need to explain how the comings and goings of pastors work in your congregation and provide a space for them to express their emotions.

If a child has had a close relationship to the pastor, perhaps an individual opportunity to say goodbye is appropriate; for those who don't need or want this, a low-key going-away party for the pastor and children might be a way to model healthy departure. Involve these children in the planning of the congregation's farewell by asking them to create artwork, poetry, music, or special gifts to give. Doing this will ensure they feel included and valued and will teach them how to say goodbye.

After the departing pastor leaves, continue to find ways to include children in the transition and the anticipation of a new pastor; don't leave them hanging with "What's next?" on their minds. Keep them informed and stay available to them. You can do this by means of an occasional dialogue with someone from the pastoral search committee during the children's time in worship; that way the adults will get to process the information too (and the kids will ask the questions the adults want to ask but won't!). Also encourage parents and learning-community teachers to talk with young ones about what is happening.

Things might unfold in the transition that you think your children and youth aren't able to process or understand given their age. The transgressions of a former pastor, for example, may not be necessary information for children to have, unless that transgression involved one or more of them. In that case, you need to create safe spaces for children to tell what they know, foremost for their own health but also so that the offender is held responsible. Responsible adults will need to make the decision about how much information kids can absorb. Don't ask children to hold confidential information, for example; the pressure of secret keeping is too great unless the secret is a special recognition or celebration. When in doubt, communicate with your children and youth; they will tell you when they've had enough, and it will lessen any sense of anxiety and awaken excitement for what is to come.

> *Invite [young people] as individuals or a group to participate in saying goodbye and later welcoming, but also in imagining new ways to minister to their community.*

High schoolers and young adults are old enough to care, be interested in, and meaningfully contribute to a congregational conversation about pastoral leadership and the season of change. Getting their time and attention is the challenge. There is a good chance they have had meaningful relationships with the outgoing pastor and have ideas about what new leadership and ministry should look like. Invite them as individuals or a group to participate in saying goodbye and later welcoming, but also in imagining new ways to minister to their community. Perhaps one or two (they likely will be more comfortable if there are two) could be invited to sit on the pastoral search committee. They will be the best bellwethers of ideas that will attract others their age. Listen to them, trust what they know, and cultivate their ideas. Allow them to show you what relevance to their age group looks, sounds, and feels like. Their engagement is a gift, and congregations would do well to nurture it in any way possible.

Not Just for Kids

Our children and youth are not the only ones who sometimes get overlooked in the conversations that happen during transitions. Other groups come to mind, those who are on the perimeter of the congregation by virtue of age, health, ability, geography, theology, or membership status. These might include folks who are homebound and in retirement or care centers, those who are differently abled, those who remain connected but live too far away to regularly participate in the day-to-day life of the congregation, those who represent a belief system outside the norm of the majority of the congregation, and those who are new members or regular visitors to the congregation.

> *Because they offer a perspective not shared by many in the congregation, finding ways to identify, engage, and genuinely listen to the people on the edges of our community life is vital.*

This goes beyond acknowledging their presence in and importance to the faith community (as mentioned when talking about the congregational profile above). What I want to emphasize here is the importance of not just having conversations *about* them, but actually having conversations *with* them. Because they offer a perspective not shared by many in the congregation, finding ways to identify, engage, and genuinely listen to the people on the edges of our community life is vital. They see, hear, interpret, and perceive in unique ways that can educate and challenge us to see our church from their experience.

Conversation with People on the Perimeter

Conversing with people on the perimeter of the congregation allows you to begin to see what they see; it's a way of expanding the view you already have, looking from the edges toward the center rather than the other way around. In addition, it is a wonderful opportunity to engage more deeply some who have been sidelined either by choice or circumstance. You will want to begin to communicate with these people as soon as possible after the announcement of the pastor's departure is made public, ensuring the news reaches them directly and promptly. Some of these folks, particularly the elderly, may have had a significant relationship with the departing pastor and may have expectations for the pastor's participation in their final years of life. Others on the periphery may not be acquainted with how pastoral transitions happen; checking in with them to educate and inform may help them feel less anxiety or confusion about what is happening. Some people on the edges are there because the only relationship they have with the church is through the pastor. Again, by extending the congregation's reach to where they are, you are reassuring them that the community as a whole values their presence.

By reaching out to these individuals, honoring their perspectives and incorporating their feedback into the overall conversation, you are communicating that you take them and their contributions seriously. It also shows them that the congregation considers them important, not just to the past but to the present and the future. For those who can change their relationship with the congregation, this might be an entrée to becoming more engaged. For those who remain on the edges, it reminds them and the congregation of their ongoing relationship and can serve to deepen that connection. Rather than seeing these folks as people "outside" of what is going on, acknowledge them and include them, seeing them as a valuable part of the whole. (For ideas about how to engage these folks, see the resources at the end of this chapter.)

Conversation with People in the Wider Community

Another group who should be intentionally included in the transforming conversation that is possible during the interim time are those who are completely outside the congregation. Why them, you may ask? Those who are not a part of our church but who share our local community are another source of insight and understanding into how the congregation is viewed in the wider community. These relationships might include our regional, judicatory, or denominational colleagues, or a neighborhood shop owner, restaurateur, or schoolteacher. By seeking out and listening closely to those in our community, we can discover fresh lenses through which to see ourselves and the world. Invite them to the conversation!

Your purpose in listening to the people in the community is to understand how others perceive the congregation and to learn what community needs are unaddressed. Someone in your denominational network would be able to tell you about how other churches view the ministry and leadership your church offers, while restaurant owners, community leaders, and neighbors could describe what they know about the church and voice questions they have about its ministry. Those living closest to the area surrounding the church could tell you what is really needed in their neighborhood; rather than assuming you know, it's always thoughtful and respectful to ask.

Inviting these people to join the conversation demonstrates the church's interest in relationships in the community. You could host a listening event, inviting nonmembers to a meal at the church, or interview them in pairs in the places where they live and work in the community. You could arrange to meet in a virtual space. Regardless of how you do it, extending the conversation that happens in the season of change into the network of relationships beyond the church's wall can provide you with insight and ideas you never considered before, as well as new ministry ideas and relationships for the future. (For additional ideas about how to engage these people, see the resources at the end of this chapter).

> *Transformation requires risking the messiness of inviting all the voices to the table.*

The Conversation Where All Are Included

The important conversations about the past and present, about leadership, relationships, and future of your congregation during the transition time are the heart of what makes change possible. When we are intentional about listening to the Spirit and about hearing God speak through others, when we design times, spaces, and ways to discern God's intent for our community with open hearts and spirits, we position ourselves to be ready for transformation. It's not enough just to gather surveys; we must engage one another in whatever way possible, face-to-face or virtually, share the joys and challenges set before us, be disturbed by the things we would rather not acknowledge, and respond to the Spirit's invitation to seek God's leading. This can't be done only in a selected series of board meetings, in a singular small group, or in a closed leadership committee. Transformation requires risking the messiness of inviting all the voices to the table.

Conversations may take place over months or a year. They may take place in homes or cafés or coffee shops, or virtually. Conversations about who your congregation is and what God is inviting you to become can take place anywhere and everywhere, as long as they respect and hold sacred the contributions of the entire people of God related to your congregation to make transformation possible.

Takeaways

- Conversations should be intentionally thoughtful, inclusive, facilitated, and honest in order to learn a congregation's truth.
- Creating opportunities for conversation about a number of areas in a church's communal life can lead to discernment and transformation.
- Conversations should include everyone in a way appropriate for their age, ability, and relationship.

Congregational Resources

A Conversation about the Past: Creating a Communal Timeline

Invite members and congregational friends to participate in creating a timeline of personal and corporate events in the history of the church. Begin by placing a long strip of paper (forty-eight-inch white or brown craft paper is perfect; newsprint sheets placed side by side can also work; an online program that helps you create a timeline will work for virtual engagement) on a wall in a prominent place in your church—the fellowship hall, narthex, or a frequently used classroom. Mark off the decades from the founding of the congregation and write in some important dates, both in history (wars, inventions, weather events) and in the life of the church (building construction, renovations and additions, pastoral leadership changes). Ask people to fill in the timeline with their personal significant events related to congregational life (membership, baptism, marriage, deaths, new ministries, mission trips, etc.) Direct people to continue to contribute over the course of several weeks, encouraging groups or individuals whose contributions seem to be missing. People who can't get to the church could send their dates into the church office, and someone could be responsible for adding them to the timeline.

Invite the congregation to a meal or worship experience focused on reviewing and celebrating the timeline you have created together. This might be the place to color code some entries: red for times the congregation remembers conflict or struggle, blue for times of transition and change, green for energy and new life. Invite conversation in small groups, asking people to reflect on where they saw or experienced God's activity across the history of the congregation (they don't need to have been there to observe trends and experiences that point to God's presence). Have them report to the whole group, marking these on the timeline. Share any other observations from the groups.

As you close, add new sections of paper labeled to capture further reflections, such as "What I hope for," "Who/What I am grateful for," "What I learned," and "What I envision." Close by giving thanks for God's faithfulness and for the faithfulness of a congregation whose life continues to unfold, even in transition.

Conversations about the Present: An Intergenerational Reality Treasure Hunt

This activity has two parts: each can be a stand-alone activity, but you will likely generate more interest, participants, and energy if you link them together.

REALITY TREASURE HUNT, PART 1: DISCOVERING OURSELVES

Recruit members of your congregation to gather information about the makeup of your current congregation. The list of information needed to be compiled could be distributed among individuals, learning-community classes, or other congregational groupings, increasing the participation across the congregation. The goal is to get an accurate picture of your congregation at the present moment, involving the most people possible in the process. (For example, a middle school class could be responsible for finding out the occupations of various members and friends of the congregation; they could do so by engaging adults in a quick conversation before or after worship, setting up a table to encourage people to write down their occupation, making up slips to go into the bulletin for people to record their answers, texting, emailing or making virtual contact.) At a minimum, you need to find out the age, gender, race/ethnicity, economic, geographic, occupational, and educational makeup of your congregation, with different people or groups responsible for each piece of the puzzle. You can also find out about the ways people serve, both in the church and the community. Finally, to get a sense of the support your congregation gives to the wider community, you might ask what organizations people contribute to financially. Could you ask the church office administrator to gather this data? Sure, but you wouldn't be building community, encouraging intergenerational conversation, and creating excitement! Set a date by which you need to gather all your data, and then ask someone to compile it by category. Part 2 comes next.

REALITY TREASURE HUNT, PART 2:
CELEBRATING OUR REFLECTION OF GOD'S IMAGE

In the second part of this activity, invite the members and friends of your congregation to compile and present the information gathered. Divide people into groups, intentionally mixing folks to achieve as much diversity as possible. (Note: It doesn't matter which group they were in to gather information or whether they participated in that process at all.) Give each group a poster board and markers and have on hand various craft supplies to be used for decorating their final projects. Having a computer and printer available would also be helpful. The goal is for each group to create a poster that represents a particular facet of the present congregation based on the facts gathered. If working virtually, assign people to breakout rooms and have one person prepared to capture the groups' ideas.

Hand out facts and ask groups to title their posters. Then give them thirty minutes to design and create an engaging poster that highlights what they learned about the congregation. Groups can decorate their artwork with the supplies available, including creating something on the computer and printing it. (Tech savvy groups could make an infographic!) Encourage creativity, such as the use of photos of people representing various age groups, colorful images, icons, graphs, charts, maps, and so on, to make their posters engaging. Provide a place where the posters can be displayed, and have each group present their poster to the whole. If groups are working virtually, spotlight each one as they present their ideas. When all the posters have been presented, ask people to share what surprises them, what strengths they see, what is missing, and what they learned from both the information and the activity.

Additional Ideas to Experiment With

- Host a game show, asking contestants to guess the information discovered by the "treasure hunt." Award fun prizes for the one who gets the most answers correct.
- Create a video presentation using free web applications that displays the information you've gathered about your congregation. This could include not only the facts but interviews with a cross section of the congregation about what they consider to be the congregation's greatest present assets.

Conversations about Leadership

The conversation about leadership should include not only who does what but an evaluation of the system currently in place. These could be combined or separate conversations.

Map the System

What does your congregation's structure look like? How is information and power restricted, shared, enhanced? Ask a couple of individuals or a group to discover the history of the organizational structure. When was the current structure put in place? What came before that? What were/are groups called and what were/are their responsibilities? What image best represents the current structure: a pyramid (note where the "wide part" is and what it represents), a circle, parallel or intersecting lines, or something else? What does this say about how power is used in the congregation?

Draw the system based on the information gathered and ask people to fill in what's missing or correct any inaccuracies. In small groups, discuss the effectiveness of the system (avoid talking about specific people here; you are assessing the *system,* not individual job holders). Where and when does it work well, disseminating information and responding to needs? Where and when does it break down, stall, or get side-tracked?

Provide the entire group with current information about what percentage of the congregation is active in leadership, works one or more jobs outside the church, and has childcare or eldercare responsibilities or other nonnegotiable time commitments. You might also consider the impact of the current trend away from people making long-term volunteer commitments and the move away from viewing religious affiliations as central to daily life.

Next ask groups to work together to imagine the most effective system for the future, based on current reality and including making space for new ministries the church wants to engage in in the future. What kind of leadership is needed? What might the leadership structure look like? How would power be used? Provide newsprint and markers and ask each group to map a revised system for the future. When the groups are finished, have them share their ideas with the entire group and discuss the merits of each suggestion. Leave the maps in a central place where others can see them as a way to continue the conversation about the church's leadership system. This can be done in person or virtually; provide paper for mapping to group leaders ahead of your gathering and then photograph each and create a slideshow to share and review their work.

CREATE A JOB FAIR

Develop a job fair to match the gifts and talents of your congregation with the jobs, responsibilities, and ministries of your congregation. Make this a part of your stewardship emphasis and encourage people to make a commitment of their time and gifts in addition to their money.

PARTICIPATION PITCH

Invite folks to participate in a speed-dating-like event where representatives of boards, committees, and ministries sit at long tables across from those who are interested in participating. Set a timer and give each rep thirty seconds to "pitch" their group to a potential participant. After time is called, potential participants move to the next seat in the line and hear a new pitch. When everyone has moved around the room back to their original spot, take a refreshment break during which people are encouraged to get more information/sign up for the board, committee, group, or ministry of their choice. This can be done virtually with timed break out rooms, an effective way to mix everyone and keep them moving.

A Conversation about Relationships beyond Ourselves

This conversation could be with a representative of a region, judicatory, or denomination, a neighborhood shop owner, restaurateur, community leader, or related organization.

WELCOME, NEIGHBOR!

Invite representatives of groups, businesses, organizations, and leadership outside your congregation for a meal and the opportunity to get to know one another better, or invite them to a virtual meeting. Tell them up front that the church is in a time of transition and is seeking to understand how they are perceived as well as become better informed about the needs of the community and how the congregation might begin to partner with others to address those needs. Ask not more than an hour of anyone's time; you want them to be interested and intrigued, not overburdened by your request. Have someone experienced in facilitating dialogue and who is a good listener lead the conversation. Ask the following questions:

- What are your perceptions about our church and its role in the community?
- Do you know anyone who attends our church?
- What do you consider to be the greatest assets of our community?
- What do you consider to be the most pressing needs of our community?
- In what ways can our congregation partner with you or others in addressing these needs?

REACHING OUT TO OUR NEIGHBORS
Instead of inviting strangers into a place where they might not be comfortable (above), reverse the process and go to them. Call ahead to make an appointment, indicating your purpose and the amount of time you expect to spend. Keep it short; fifteen to twenty minutes is a good place to start. Send people out in pairs (disciple-style; see earlier suggestions) to interview folks using the questions above, written out for one person to ask while the other records the responses provided. Bring relevant information about your church to share with the person, and be gracious and generous in your appreciation for the time they have given you. This could be the beginning of a new or deeper relationship!

A Conversation about the Future

SPIRITUAL AND SOCIAL ENTREPRENEURSHIP: IMAGINATION EXPLORATION
As you consider the future of your congregation, use the data you have acquired about your congregation and your wider community to brainstorm possible new ministries and outreach you might explore during this transitional season in the life of your church. This exercise can take some time, so if people are willing to commit to the process, you could divide it up and give them homework, asking them to return to the conversation a second time to complete their work. Allow about ninety minutes per

session, keeping watch on the time and moving the groups along through the process.

Invite people to a conversation about the future with the goal of stimulating their imaginations about possible new ministries for your congregation to try out during the interim time. Begin by listing known challenges in your neighborhood and wider community; these may have come from previous conversations with people on the perimeter, people and organizations the congregation is related to outside the church, or information gleaned from wider community discussion or recent events. Be sure you are dealing in real, not simply perceived, problems.

Place a piece of newsprint on each table with one of the identified challenges at the top and invite people to self-select the problem they would like to think about. Ask them to do the following things, in this order:

1. Identify the problem as specifically as possible: Whom does this affect? How many does this affect? What results because of this problem?
2. Determine the root causes of the problem: where did this start? When did this start? What is it related to? (Dig deep here; root causes often go back decades, even centuries! Try to probe as deeply as possible, making as many connections as required to get to the heart of the origin of the problem.)
   (*If you are going to make this a two-meeting process, end session 1 here and give people step 3 as their homework assignment. They can return with that information and begin by sharing it with their group.*)
3. Who is currently doing what to address the problem? (Some internet work here can be helpful.) Find examples of who is attempting to address all or part of this issue locally, regionally, and beyond.
4. Assess the positives and negatives of these current efforts. Identify what is working and what is being left undone.
5. Brainstorm all the unique possibilities that could be used to address even a small piece of this challenge. The key here is "unique"! Think *way* outside the box! (I tell

people that as long as it's not illegal or immoral, put it on the brainstorm list!) Invoke God's creative imagination to dream up something new! Give each group member some sticky notes and have them write down ideas as quickly as they come, one per note, and stick those notes on a sheet of newsprint. Don't discuss ideas; just stick them on the paper. Nothing is too outrageous; trust God to inspire!

6. When the brainstorming is exhausted, have the group read their notes to one another and group like ideas together on the paper. Get clarification on the basics of an idea if necessary.

7. When each idea has been described adequately for the group, without further discussion, ask each person to "vote" by placing a check mark or star by their top three choices.

8. Tabulate the votes and list three or four ideas with the most votes on a clean piece of newsprint.

9. Talk about your choices and have each group member vote again, choosing their most interesting idea.

10. Write your new idea on a clean sheet of newsprint.

What happens next? You have a unique idea that at least a small group of people are interested in! Use this as a starting place for further conversations about future ministry. You could try the following:

- Schedule another congregational event and host a *Shark Tank*–like pitch session where individuals or groups can pitch their ideas to the entire congregation and see who would like to sign on to explore the possibilities of each.
- As a congregation, choose one idea that you would like to explore further, and gather a group of interested persons to develop the idea, including creating a possible timeline with goals to complete in the coming year. Be sure to identify measurable outcomes so that you can gauge your success and make adjustments if you want to continue beyond your first attempt.

- If you want to do this exercise online there are many free applications available to make this a series of virtual events using platforms such as Zoom, PowerPoint, Google Docs/Slides and Canva.

A Kids Conversation about Transition and Transformation

This conversation could take place during worship or in a children's learning environment. In preparation, prepare two signs big enough to hold up; one should say "Transition" and one should say "Transformation."

Gather the "kids" in a comfortable spot. (In my invitation, "kids" includes whoever wants to come.) In a traditional worship space, it's usually in the front of the worship space; one congregation I worshiped in had a "kids' corner" in the back of the sanctuary, so the person engaging the children went there to talk to the young ones during worship. I usually like to sit on the floor with them or have them sit on a pew facing me; the important thing is that I sit at their level.

Adult: Hi everyone! [If you can call them by name, even better; take your time. They will love to help you as well as test you!] I want to talk to you today about something that's happening in our church, and I want to use two *t* words to do it. Can anyone tell me what this *t* word is? (*Hold up a sign that says "transition."*)

Kids: (*Some are uncertain; one or more reads, "Transition."*)

Adult: Great! Does anyone know what that means?

Kids: (*An older kid might give a response; a younger one might not have a response on target.*) A change?

Adult: A transition is a change. Suppose I take this hymnal (*taking it from the pew*) and put it over here. Is that a transition? What has changed?

Kids: You moved it. So yeah, I guess it's a transition.

Adult: But not much has changed, right? I just moved this book from here to there. It's still the same book; it's just in a different place. Okay, let's look at my second *t* word. (*Show them.*) What does this one say?

Kids: Transformation.

Adult: What does that mean?

Kids: (*This is harder, so you might get more puzzled looks. You might get an answer that's close or something completely out of the ballpark. Just go with it! Acknowledge each try.*)

Adult: That's a good try: anyone else?

Kids: (*They may try again or may be completely baffled*).

Adult: Let me help you. A transformation is when something changes so much that it's hard to recognize it's the same thing. It looks almost completely different. Can you think of any examples of things that do transformations?

Kids: (*Give them a chance to think; older kids might have a response. Younger ones won't likely get it right away. Be patient.*)

Adult: (*Hold up a packet of seeds.*) What are these?

Kids: Seeds.

Adult: What would happen if I put them in good soil, watered them, and left them in the sunshine?

Kids: They would grow into something.

Adult: Right! They would grow into this flower! (*Show them a picture.*) Does this (*show seed*) look like this (*show flower*)?

Kids: No!

Adult: It's a transformation! The seed didn't just change a little; it changed a lot! It doesn't even look like the seed it started from. Can you think of other things that start off as one thing and become another different-looking thing?

Kids: (*Give kids a chance to respond; some might have answers; they might mention the toy Transformers that change from action figures to vehicles, for example.*)

Adult: Ice transforms when it melts into a puddle; caterpillars transform when they turn into butterflies; milk, cream, and sugar transform into ice cream. Sometimes bullies can transform into friends and people who are sad can transform into people who are happy. Anyone can transform when we realize how deeply God loves and cares for us and we, in turn, love others!

Adult: (*continuing*) We love our church, and we are praying that God will not just "transition" us, move us from one place to another, but that God will "transform" us as we learn to love God and one another more and more each day. We want what we do and say to look and sound more and more like Jesus. Can you think of a way we can do this?

Kids: (*maybe*) Be nicer? Help people. Pray.

Adult: All those things are ways God can begin to transform us. God can take who and what our church is right now and make us into a whole new church to love and serve God and our neighbors. And you are a part of that! So I want to invite you to pray with me and learn with me. Let's help one another transform into who and what God imagines us to be! Let's pray together right now!

    Thank you, God, for the seed, the water, even being sad. Each one is important, and each can transform into something else. Help us to be transformed into kids and adults who act and sound more and more like Jesus every day, sharing your love with one another and everyone we meet. Amen.

A Conversation with Someone on the Perimeter

This could be with those who are on the perimeter of the congregation by virtue of age, health, ability, geography, theology, membership status, or something else.

Invite people who are comfortable reaching out to others to reach out to someone who is on the perimeter of the congregation. They may invite them to coffee or tea, call them on the phone, take them to lunch, or just find a quiet corner to talk before or after a church event. The following questions might guide the conversation:

- What questions can I answer or information can I give you regarding our pastoral transition?
- Will you tell me about how you became acquainted with our church?
- How are you feeling about your connection to our church at the present time? Would you like to become more connected? If yes, how could I help to facilitate that? If not, could you tell why not so we can learn more about you and ourselves as a church?
- As we experience this season of transition, is there anything that you hope will happen or that you think should be addressed during this time?
- What kind of pastoral leader do you think our congregation should seek for the future?
- Is there anything we can do to support or encourage you? Is there anything we can pray with you about?
- May I share your thoughts and ideas as a part of our communal conversation?
- Thank them for their time and their contribution to the conversation. Assure them that things they have asked to remain confidential will be respected and things they will allow to be shared will be included.

Note

1. Christel Temple, "The Emergence of *Sankofa* Practice in the United States: A Modern History," *Journal of Black Studies* 41, no. 1 (September 2010): 127.

CHAPTER FOUR

SPECIAL MUSIC

They Are Singing Our Song

Music in worship invites us to hear God's voice and experience the movement of the Spirit in a unique way. Through the use of instrumental or vocal music, we tap into different resources than we generally access when we are listening to words or speaking ourselves.

Special music in worship is more than just a break in the action or opportunity to check our cell phones. It is a pause in the routine of worship that invites us to open ourselves to hearing God in a fresh and creative way. Instead of a choir, it might be an instrumental or vocal soloist. Instead of an organ, it might be a guitar. Instead of congregational voices, it might feature a duet or quartet; instead of a piano, there might be a trumpet, flute, or stringed instrument. It may also spotlight the gifts of guest artists or of church members who aren't part of the regular music ministry. We call it "special" because it is outside our normal expectation, because it invites us, by design, to contemplate the intersection of God's presence and our experience of the Holy in a unique moment.

In the same way, we can expand how we consider and embrace transition in our lives and in the church by listening to the voices of those *outside* the church who have studied human, natural, and institutional behavior and whose work can add meaning and clarity to our self-understanding. When we add these unique voices to what we already know, we create space for God's "special music" to take root in us and our minds are expanded in preparation to hear God's Word.

Familiar Tune, New Words

William Bridges, considered by many to be the "preeminent authority on change,"[1] is one such voice. Focused on businesses in transition, Bridges's understanding of human nature in response to change grounds his work and speaks to all of us who experience transition, whether we are a congregation of fewer than fifty people or a multimillion-dollar corporation with thousands of employees. There are things about change that affect us all similarly; knowledge of these common responses and impulses both normalizes our reactions and gives us clues as to how best to manage transitions.

> *The failure to identify and get ready for endings and losses is the largest difficulty for people in transition. And the failure to provide help with endings and losses leads to more problems for organizations in transition than anything else.* —William Bridges

In his work, Bridges maps the landscape of change by describing three distinct movements. Transition begins with an ending, with loss and letting go, followed by what he calls the neutral zone, and it concludes with a new beginning. He diagrams it in such a way that these processes overlap; "letting go" continues to happen even as we shift into "neutral," and the "beginning" is started even as we continue letting go.[2] The most important part of the change process, according to Bridges, is how we end something—a way of operating, relationships with a leader, a particular ministry or task. "The failure to identify and get ready for endings and losses is the largest difficulty for people in transition. And the failure to provide help with endings and losses leads to more problems for organizations in transition than anything else."[3]

Healthy transition starts with an ending: the pastor is leaving or has already left. Bridges's work suggests that rather than hurry to fill the role and ease our discomfort, attending to our feelings and experiences from this moment and continuing until the next leader is called is important work; it must not be minimized or covered over. Allowing ourselves to process this change and what it means is central to our personal and congregational health as we move into the next season of our lives together.

> *The first task of transition management is to convince people to leave home.* —William Bridges

The problem with change, asserts Bridges, is that people don't like it![4] Even if we aren't happy with the way things are, many of us would rather settle for what is familiar than exert the effort necessary to make meaningful change. It's important that we recognize who has lost what, acknowledge those losses openly, expect and recognize the signs of grieving over our losses, and treat the past with respect.[5] Helping people to name these experiences helps them to have a sense of control over them. Giving them language that honors the past as a foundation for the future promotes a sense of continuity and recognizes the legacy of past leaders. Bridges puts the season of letting go this way: "The first task of *transition management* is to convince people to leave home."[6] It is in our ability and willingness to "leave home," giving up what is familiar, comfortable, and sure, that makes it possible to transition toward the future.

Even as we are still processing the ending of our past reality, we move into the "neutral zone." Bridges describes this space as a "psychological no-man's-land."[7] It's that liminal place between what was and what is yet to be. It's a place of uncertainty but also of exploration. It's a place of wonder and a place of imagination, of listening to God and one another and discovering our faithful response. Again, many are tempted to rush through this season to find more certain, stable ground. But without this time in the neutral zone, questions don't get asked, assumptions aren't challenged, holy imaginations aren't stirred, and we might never know what God has in store! For Bridges, the neutral zone is the "core" of the transition process; it is both a "dangerous and opportune place."[8] It is *dangerous* because this is the time when people's anxieties are heightened, motivation falls, we become overloaded with responsibilities,[9] and in the church, many take the opportunity to leave.

> *The neutral zone is the "core" of the transition process; it is both a "dangerous and opportune place." —William Bridges*

Bridges likens the neutral zone to the experience of the Israelites wandering in the wilderness. Old connections, ideas, habits, and relationships must "die off" before people are prepared for new ones. A prolonged time between what was and what is to be allows us to shed the things of the past that we do not need and strengthen ourselves with what we do need. Forty years is certainly longer than your average pastoral transition period will last, although there may be times when it seems like decades have passed! The neutral zone "is a time when reorientation and redefinition must take place, and people need to understand that."[10] Perhaps we can think of the neutral zone as the lyrical bridge or musical interlude that begins to turn our hearts and minds to God's future and live into what is possible for us as individuals and as the church.

But notice that even as Bridges describes the neutral zone as being dangerous, he also sees it as opportune. It's a time to deepen our experience of the Holy. It's the time to begin to learn a new song! Discern and experiment with God's invitation to the future. Encourage people to claim their gifts, try new leadership positions, and explore new ministries as they clarify who they are as individuals and as the body of Christ together. As the need to adapt to something new in the absence of past leadership becomes more apparent, reframe this season as a time to be creative, a time to risk and try, a time to learn and wonder as you set your sights on the future. You may discover that you don't need to wait for a permanent settled pastor for new life to begin! You can start singing now!

Adding Another Voice

Margaret Wheatley is an author who captured my imagination many years ago and who continues to influence leaders around the world by integrating scientific and social thought to help us understand how and why change happens in the natural world as well as in our own lives. Wheatley has authored many books, but the one that has spoken most to me about my experience with transition in the church is titled *Leadership and the New Science: Learning about Organization from an Orderly Universe*.[11] Here she demonstrates the correlation between naturally occurring change and our own need to be open to the possibilities that transitions offer us.

Arguing that change is normal and, in fact, the basis for creativity in the universe, Wheatley invites us to apply the rules of quantum theory (yes, really!) to our everyday experiences. She argues that in the quantum understanding of the universe, everything is in relationship to everything else; reducing matter to parts and functions creates a false reality. Because everything is in relationship, each element, each thing, living and nonliving, has an effect on another. When we are in relationship, our lives change when the people and things around us change. That's both the beauty and challenge of community and living in the natural world; we can't control our situation. When we resist change in ourselves or others, we are attempting to stop or limit the very nature of how the universe works.

> *Change and transition must be allowed to happen, even embraced as it is happening, for us to participate in creation and recreation of new expressions of life.*

By holding on to the past, by resisting change, we actually are resisting the motion and work of God's creation! Wheatley says, "I've observed the search for organizational equilibrium as a sure path to institutional death, a road to zero trafficked by fearful people."[12] In other words, trying to maintain the way our churches functioned in the past, with the leadership of the past, is a movement toward organizational death, not life. Change must be allowed to happen, even embraced as it is happening, for us to participate in creation and recreation of new expressions of life, even and perhaps especially, in the church.

If we really believe that God's Spirit is alive within and among us, *moving* us to new understandings of God, ourselves, and the world, then we should *welcome* the instability of transition as an indicator of life! "To stay viable, open systems maintain a state of non-equilibrium, keeping the system off balance so that it can change and grow,"[13] Wheatley explains. Openness to one another, openness to God's Spirit, intentionally entering into a season of discernment and possibility are what make transformation *possible*. Without this freedom, without this creative space, we extinguish the possibility of life that can emerge within and among us.

Like a glaringly wrong note in a chord, this idea of inviting destabilization in order to grow seems counterintuitive, for sure. Churches in particular are noted for their propensity to rely on the past as an indicator of the future. From "We've always done it that way" to "Back when we had two hundred kids in Sunday school," we look back with longing, hoping to find the fix that will replicate the successes of yesterday. In one congregation I served, my pastoral partner[14] and I used to intentionally put forward a controversial topic for occasional congregational meetings simply to change up the "music," to keep people thinking and discerning the revelation and call of God in their midst.

Those who are wise enough to notice that the present looks and acts nothing like the past may yet resist change in hopes of holding on to what might still be working today. But that is no guarantee for tomorrow. Stability isn't the answer, according to Wheatley. Nothing in the universe is stable! Self-renewing systems are distinguished by resiliency, not stability.[15] We can be "self-renewing" if we are motivated by the ever-present creative Spirit of God who is at work in us; trust in that Spirit is what gives us the resiliency we need, the ability to adapt, show flexibility, and embrace change. When we are pushed out of our comfort zones, it is a wise, creative, resilient God who leads our transformation.

> It's important to recognize that change and transformation are not the same.

Singing a New Song

Using very different starting places, both Bridges and Wheatley point us toward the end goal: transformation, new life. Their "song" may be unfamiliar, but both point to the human and

natural world, God's world, and invite us to replicate what we
know about ourselves and the context we live in to inform and
guide our way. It's important to recognize that change and transformation are not the same. Change is an external effort to do
something differently; for example, we decide to worship on Sat-
urday night rather than Sunday morning. Transformation is an
internal shift in how we know and define ourselves; for instance,
we are compelled to move beyond the confines of our church
building to address the needs of the community in which we live.
Change is not necessarily bad, but it is also not lasting. Transformation reorients us to God and to God's world permanently. It is
expressed in living out a new understanding of ourselves and our
witness to become disciples of Jesus in the world. Both Bridges
and Wheatley point us toward transformation. In doing so, they
affirm that the timing of new life is organic; we can't orchestrate
it. Just because we call a new pastor, new life is not guaranteed.
Transformation happens most profoundly when it emerges out of
experimentation (Bridges) and chaos (Wheatley).

> *Change is an external effort to do something differently. Transforma-*
> *tion is an internal shift in how we know and define ourselves.*

New life can't be coerced or forced, warns Bridges. It is "organic," growing out of informed opportunities for change. We
can, however, influence it; we can encourage growth, support
change, and reinforce new understandings of ourselves and the
world.[16] We can change the music! Wheatley adds that not only is
transformation organic, but it is chaotic; yet while particles (and
people!) may act in unpredictable order, they replicate a dominant
pattern. These are the guiding principles that serve to organize
particles and influence their behavior.[17] From these observations,
Wheatley concludes, "But if we can trust the workings of chaos,
we will see that the dominant shape of our organization can be
maintained if we retain clarity about the purpose and direction of
the organization."[18]

What does this mean for the congregation in transition? It
means that if we can remain committed to our faith in God and
our call to discipleship, then our communal values and dedication

to this purpose will guide us through the "chaos" of the transitional time to wholeness, to new life. We must trust that the God who created the wild and wonderfully diverse universe that acts in this way will replicate that action on our own lives and communities. Transformation is possible! Uncertainty can and will give way to a new way of being, a new way of experiencing God, a new song to sing!

Let's return to Bridges one more time; he provides some concrete steps to help people navigate the confusion and chaos of transition. His alliteration helps us to remember the things he considers essential for transformation: *purpose*, *picture*, *plan*, and *part*.[19] It's important for people to understand what is happening; when a pastor leaves, we gain the trust and confidence of others by explaining as clearly as possible what is happening and why. Share your *purpose* with your congregation: to continue to serve God and your community in faithfulness as you look toward the future. You can help people to understand what the next season will look like with a scriptural metaphor, a *picture* of what the future might offer. (See chapter 5, "The Word in Words.") Bridges returns to his use of the account of the Israelites in the wilderness to help people envision the future as life giving, the "land of milk and honey."[20] Tell your congregation the *plan* for getting there, as you know it and as it unfolds. Shared information is shared power; people need to know what is going to happen so they can support one another. That allows them to take *part* in the process, both in embracing their relationships with one other and in taking a role in creating God's future.[21]

Everybody Sing

Music allows us to give voice and expression to the creative movement of God's Spirit in our midst; it has the power both to transport us out of and deeply into ourselves and to respond emotionally, spiritually, and physically to the divine presence we experience. Adding the wisdom of other voices to our own deepens our pool of knowledge and widens our understanding and appreciation. Both music and learning can be transformative; open hearts and minds can make every spirit sing!

Takeaways

- Listening to the voices of those *outside* the church who have studied human, natural, and institutional behavior and work can add meaning and clarity to our self-understanding inside the church.
- Bridges describes transition as beginning with an ending, with loss and letting go, followed by the "neutral zone" and concluding with a new beginning. He diagrams it in such a way that these processes overlap.
- The failure to provide help with endings and losses leads to more problems for organizations in transition than anything else. (Bridges)
- The neutral zone can be both a dangerous and opportune time and space. (Bridges)
- All things are in relationship; a shift in one effects a change in another (Wheatley).
- Destabilization causes us to grow (Wheatley).
- Change is external; transformation is internal.
- Faithfulness to God serves as a strong organizing principle that can guide transition.

Congregational Resources

Conversation Questions

You might use these questions in an adult Sunday school or learning community class, a board or committee meeting, or any other group as you check in with one another about the process of transition.

1. In what ways does music affect your sense of worship and your experience of God? Recall a time when music was particularly meaningful to you.
2. Which phase of Bridges's description of transition (loss and letting go, neutral zone, new beginning) best describes where you experience yourself at this time? Where do you think the congregation is at this time?

3. Describe the type of music that accompanies your sense of where you find yourself in your answer to question 2.

4. In her book *Leadership and the New Science*, Wheatley explores the science behind interrelatedness. All things in nature are relational. Describe your own sense of connectedness to this congregation in the past and present. What would you hope for the future? What does your connectedness look like? How is it tied to your relationship with God?

5. Bridges argues that healthy endings are the most important part of the transition process. What is your life experience with endings? How are you feeling about the endings in your church? How do healthy endings contribute to healthy new beginnings?

6. Wheatley understands that destabilization is necessary for newness to emerge. Describe a time when you experienced a situation or relationship destabilized (shaky, uncertain, not going the way you had predicted); what was the outcome? What is it about destabilization that helps us move forward?

7. Think about your congregation and the difference between change and transformation. Which do you see your congregation doing now or in the future? What might be the benefits and limitations of change? Of transformation? How can you invite God into the process of discerning what is necessary in your church?

8. What "song" (literal or figurative) do you wish your church could sing?

Quotes to Ponder

You might use these quotes as a starting place for a conversation about transformation in your congregation. You could also include them in your bulletin or newsletter, place one on your website, or write a blog or article with a quote as your starting point. The idea is to get people thinking and talking about change.

- "In any significant transition, the thing that the organization needs to let go of is the very thing that got it this far."[22]
- "Your history can block your future, or it can give you a foundation for your future. You can stay focused on what you used to be . . . or you can use that history like a launching pad."[23]
- "There is no power equal to a community discovering what it cares about."[24]
- "Change always starts with confusion; cherished interpretations must dissolve to make way for the new. Of course, it's scary to give up what we know, but the abyss is where newness lives. Great ideas and inventions miraculously appear in the space of not knowing. If we can move through the fear and enter the abyss, we are rewarded greatly. We rediscover we are creative."[25]

Songs to Sing

During the transition season, you can use the power of music to convey hope, courage, anticipation, and faithfulness. You might consider these ideas:

- **Meaningful Music:** Ask members of a particular group to choose a song that is most meaningful to them during transitions because of the words, tune, or both. Have people bring a copy of the lyrics for the group to read and discuss and listen to the music (you will find many recorded renditions of all types of music, including hymns, online). Consider what each particular piece speaks to in a time of transition and transformation.
- **New Expressions:** Invite different musical expressions to be shared over the course of a season or monthly during your time of transition. Use people, groups, instruments, styles you don't usually hear (or hear in church), if possible. Frame this as an opportunity to listen for God's voice through a fresh medium. Ask people not to critique

the music but rather to consider how they "heard" God in a new way.

- **Create a Theme Song:** Choose a theme song that speaks to your congregation about their experience of change and their hope of transformation. Sing/listen to it weekly at the beginning or close of each service or gathering. Add verses of your own: recruit children, youth, young adults, older adults, and other groups to write a verse so that you can swap them out and create your own musical journey together.

- **Enter the Stillness:** Create a regular opportunity for quiet in your congregation. Set aside a small space that could be used for contemplation, prayer, or silent meditation. Introduce quiet to the worship service (so often we insist on filling space with our own voices!). This could include some soft instrumental music in the background to help people find quiet. Help people enter into this time by giving them a brief Scripture, simple phrase to repeat: "Enter my heart, O God" or "I am loved by God," and "Be still, and know that I am God!" (Psalm 46:10) are simple but effective prayers.

Notes

1. William Bridges with Susan Bridges, *Managing Transitions: Making the Most of Change*, 4th ed. (Boston: Da Capo, 2016), back cover.

2. Bridges and Bridges, 5.

3. Bridges and Bridges, 8.

4. Bridges and Bridges, 27.

5. Bridges and Bridges, 29–40.

6. Bridges and Bridges, 42.

7. Bridges and Bridges 9.

8. Bridges and Bridges, 10.

9. Bridges and Bridges, 46–47.

10. Bridges and Bridges, 49.

11. I am referencing the 1994 edition here; there is a later edition with a similar yet different title.

12. Margaret Wheatley, *Leadership and the New Science: Learning about Organization from an Orderly Universe* (San Francisco: Berrett-Koehler, 1994), 76.

13. Wheatley, 78.

14. *Pastoral partner* is a term we coined to describe the coequal relationship and responsibilities we shared with each other as pastoral leaders and with the congregation.

15. Wheatley, *Leadership and the New Science*, 88.

16. Bridges and Bridges, *Managing Transitions*, 68.

17. Wheatley, *Leadership and the New Science*, 132.

18. Wheatley, 133.

19. Bridges and Bridges, *Managing Transitions*, 68.

20. Bridges and Bridges, 73.

21. Bridges and Bridges, 76.

22. Bridges and Bridges, 96.

23. Loren B. Mead, *A Change of Pastors . . . and How It Affects Change in the Congregation* (Herndon, VA: Alban Institute, 2005), 51.

24. Margaret Wheatley, *Turning to One Another: Simple Conversations to Restore Hope to the Future*, 2nd ed. (San Francisco: Berrett-Koehler, 2009), 22.

25. Wheatley, *Turning to One Another*, 37.

CHAPTER FIVE

THE WORD IN WORDS

The Word for Us

The reading of the biblical text, God's Word for us, and the preaching of the text, our words about God, are central to many Protestant worship services. Laying aside the variety of ways we understand and interpret scripture, what I suspect we find most unifying and compelling in the biblical story is its timelessness in speaking to our feelings and the lived universal human experience. This is true for the seasons of transition and potential transformation as well. We can ground ourselves and our experience of searching for, and saying goodbye and welcome to, pastoral leaders in ancient stories of transitions. Seeking and finding, wonder and confusion, uncertainty and loss, hungering for new life and hope are not unique to us or to our time.

In spite of that reality, I struggled for a long time trying to find the "perfect" biblical text to speak to this transitional season of a congregation's life until I finally realized that just as there are many ways to experience a change in pastoral leadership, so there are many biblical examples and assurances that can accompany us on that journey. Finding the ones that best fit your congregation's experience will rely in part on your understanding of where you are and how you got there. The rest you can trust to the Holy Spirit.

Biblical Communities in Transition

Many books written for transitional pastors suggest that the quintessential interim story is that of the people of Israel wandering in the desert in search of the Promised Land. Beginning in Exodus 13:17, we are told of a people physically freed from the past but facing a decidedly uncertain future. With Moses standing in as the "transitional pastor," we can follow the biblical text all the way to the transfer of authority to the next leader, Joshua, as Moses gives up his role in deference to the one called by God and affirmed by the people.

> *It reminds us of God's enduring faithfulness when we cannot see where the path will lead; it assures us that God will call and prepare a leader for the future.*

Seeing this account as a time of transition is a powerful lens through which to examine both this story and our own. I have used it myself in my first few months of pastoral leadership in transitioning congregations. Loss, looking back with longing, uncertainty, the rise of challenging feelings like anger and discouragement, as well as experiencing hope and anticipation, are all a significant part of the "wandering" narrative. This account reminds us of God's enduring faithfulness when we cannot see where the path will lead; it assures us that God will call and prepare a leader for the future. Just because it is used frequently in transition ministries does not mean it doesn't warrant continued use! If you can see yourself and your congregation in this story, then hear it anew through the lens of pastoral change.

Another communal transition story that is central to the biblical text is the transition Jesus' disciples experienced as he prepared them for his death and resurrection and for the gift of the Holy Spirit. In all four Gospels, Jesus spoke to his followers about what lay ahead, yet they did not fully understand his meaning. After Jesus' resurrection, they grieved his loss for a second time, but he assured them that with the help of the Holy Spirit, the ministry would continue and they would be empowered to lead it (Acts

1:6-8). Following the story from the Gospels into the Acts of the Apostles, we see how this empowerment transformed both the disciples and the community (Acts 2:1-36). New leaders arose: Matthias (Acts 1:23-26), Peter (Acts 2:14-24, 38-41; 3:6-7), Paul (Acts 9:1-9), Phoebe (Romans 16:1-2) and the other women in ministry in Rome (Romans 16:3-16), and indeed the gospel continues to effect change in all who hear its liberating message. This transition story is a powerful reminder of God's faithfulness to the entire community in the midst of dramatic, ongoing change.

Biblical Leadership in Transition

The biblical text has many stories of leaders in transition, some that turned out to be successful and some that didn't. Many of these stories tell of succession leadership, which is the name given for what happens when the previous leader selects and trains the next leader to take their place (discussed in its contemporary expression in chapter 1, "Call to Worship"). This was the way ancient rulers and monarchs were selected, so it is not surprising then that ancient faith communities adopted the same model. While today this is primarily a strategy used in business, there is currently a renewed interest in this kind of leadership selection in some religious traditions where it has not been used, even while in traditions where it has been the accepted practice, others are moving away from succession leadership. What's this about?

> *Many of these stories tell of succession leadership, which is the name given for what happens when the previous leader selects and trains the next leader to take their place.*

Those for whom succession leadership is new seem to be looking for a way to ease the pain and potential loss of momentum during the transition process by having the two pastoral leaders— outgoing and incoming—overlap. The outgoing pastor could be the former settled pastor or the transitional pastor, if there is one. The intent is to make the move between the two leaders less disruptive to the life and ministry of the congregation. While this may seem appealing, it requires that a congregation be able to afford to pay two pastors' salaries for a predetermined time period. If, instead of paying two pastors full-time, the church decides to have them both serve at half-time, it also requires that the pastors find themselves able to live on a partial salary while they either ramp up or down and that they find a way to divide the leadership roles that won't also create divisions in the congregation.

What I don't see happening here is the intentional reflection on the five major areas of focus for transition ministry (reflecting on a congregation's history, defining the makeup and values of the present congregation, understanding congregational patterns of leadership, evaluating and affirming relationships beyond the congregation, and thinking about the future, all described in detail in appendix B) unless the outgoing pastor is the transitional minister. This work can't happen effectively with the previous pastor.

> *Outgoing pastors in this tradition can cement their legacy of goodwill with the congregation by giving them the freedom to seek God's direction as they discern their future.*

So why are some congregations who have been using the succession model moving away from it? Because in many of these congregations, the pastor's choice of the next leader has excluded the work of intentional reflection and transition and has had the tendency to limit the potential new leaders to those of the current pastor's protégés or friend circle. In some cases, the new leader is chosen for their ability to replicate the previous pastor's style and priorities, without giving the congregation effective voice, discernment, and decision-making power in the process. These congregations are discovering the value in having a transitional pastor who will work with them through the challenges of change and who will support their autonomy in choosing their own pastoral leader based on the future they envision rather than on the past. Outgoing pastors in this tradition can cement their legacy of goodwill with the congregation by giving them the freedom to seek God's direction as they discern their future.

If you want to consider the biblical leaders who came to authority with the succession model of leadership transference, there are several in the Bible. The Hebrew scriptures especially reflect this model, which mimicked the political model of leadership in the same time period. You would want to consider how Moses prepared Joshua (Numbers 27:12-23; Deuteronomy 31), or how Elijah prepared Elisha (1 Kings 19; 2 Kings 2). Eli attempted to prepare his sons, but they turned out to be failures where leadership was concerned (1 Samuel 2:12-17, 22-25); Samuel, the son of Elkanah and Hannah, however, turned out to be God's choice to succeed Eli (1 Samuel 3).

A bit more abstractly, in the New Testament we could point to Jesus' commissioning of the disciples after his resurrection as "successor" stories: the gathered followers found Jesus among them and were told that he was sending them (Mark 16:15; Luke 24:49); the women who encountered the risen Christ at the tomb were told to tell others (Matthew 28:7; Mark 16:7; Luke 24:9); Peter, encountering Jesus on the beach, was told to "feed my sheep" (John 21:17). And all of the disciples, by the authority of Jesus himself, were exhorted to "go therefore and make disciples of all nations" (Matthew 28:18-19). "As the Father has sent me, so I send you" (John 20:21). Finally, it was the apostle Paul who trained and gave authority to Timothy, another "successor" found in the biblical text (2 Timothy 4:1-2).

Finally, don't pass over John the Baptizer as a model transitional leader. He had no agenda but to prepare people to encounter Jesus. He came infused with divine blessing, holding up the prophetic proverbial mirror for a community whose religious life had been corrupted by greed and politics (Matthew 3; Mark 1:1-8; Luke 3:1-18; John 1:19-34). John sought only to orient people toward the true leader, Jesus. His prophetic voice awakened people to their need for a new relationship with God.

Biblical Words of Transformation

Many years ago, a friend and mentor of mine, Ron Morgan, shared an experience of his own transformation. Bearing witness to the economic and physical suffering of the people of El Salvador, he found his heart breaking. How could he return to his privileged North American life when so many were in such deep poverty and anguish? How could he incorporate what he saw and felt with his faith in a loving, compassionate God? It was in this struggle that he came to clarity about the difference between being "broken" and "broken open." When we are "broken," we are taken apart, dismantled in some way (my words, not his), and are never the same again. Such devastating brokenness often leads to dysfunction and the inability to continue to be who and what we have been. But being "broken open" is an entirely different experience.

We are "broken open," he discovered, so that we can be made into something new. To be "broken open," we must make ourselves vulnerable. We must be willing to sacrifice our carefully constructed facades that mask the confusion, hurt, and pain we hold within. While "breaking" can shatter us, "breaking open" can transform us! Risking vulnerability, we open ourselves to a new understanding and vision of others, ourselves, and the world in the redeeming mercy of God in Christ. While transition can lead us from one place to another, it does not require that we change to get there. Transformation, on the other hand, invites us to be "broken open" to reveal God's potential hidden deep within. Your congregation, with the grace of the Holy Spirit, can choose to experience transition or transformation in the process of transition, but you must be willing to be vulnerable in order to be made new.

While "breaking" can shatter us, "breaking open" can transform us!

Many biblical passages invite this kind of emotional, psychological, spiritual change, some overlapping those we have already mentioned. The story of Jacob wrestling with the angel in the night (Genesis 32:22-31), Esther rising to leadership in response to the need of the moment (Esther 4:9-17), the Samaritan woman speaking with Jesus at the well (John 4:7-30), and the disciples conversing with Jesus on the Emmaus road (Luke 24:13-27) come quickly to mind, all accounts of individuals who were "broken open," who were transformed. But the experience of transformation is not given to just a few; it is God's invitation to us all:

> Do not remember the former things,
>   or consider the things of old.
> I am about to do a new thing;
>   now it springs forth, do you not perceive it?
> I will make a way in the wilderness
>   and rivers in the desert.
>   —Isaiah 43:18-19

Recall also the prophet Ezekiel's conversation with God in the valley of dry bones:

> He said to me, "Mortal, can these bones live?" I answered, "O Lord GOD, you know." Then he said to me, "Prophesy to these bones and say to them: O dry bones, hear the word of the LORD. Thus says the Lord GOD to these bones: I will cause breath to enter you, and you shall live. I will lay sinews on you, and will cause flesh to come upon you, and cover you with skin, and put breath in you, and you shall live; and you shall know that I am the Lord." (Ezekiel 37:3-6)

New wine needing new wineskins is a powerful image of transformation:

> No one sews a piece of unshrunk cloth on an old cloak, for the patch pulls away from the cloak, and a worse tear is made. Neither is new wine put into old wineskins; otherwise, the skins burst, and the wine is spilled, and the skins are destroyed; but new wine is put into fresh wineskins, and so both are preserved. (Matthew 9:16-17)

Romans 12 speaks not only of the need to be transformed but describes the vulnerability necessary to accomplish it:

> I appeal to you therefore, brothers and sisters, by the mercies of God, to present your bodies as a living sacrifice, holy and acceptable to God, which is your spiritual worship. Do not be conformed to this world, but be transformed by the renewing of your minds, so that you may discern what is the will of God— what is good and acceptable and perfect. (Romans 12:1-2)

Many other verses of scriptures (some found at the end of this chapter) call us to transformation, as both individuals and as the community of Christ together. Making these the focus of your worship, preaching, study, and prayer can encourage the kind of spiritual growth and movement that allows us, not to be broken, but to be *broken open* so that we might experience transformation in the midst of pastoral change.

God's Word in Our Words

That God's Word speaks to us across generations in every aspect of our lives is an amazing gift. That we sometimes fail to hear it in our own context is a loss on our part. We can be true to the biblical context and apply its teaching to our lives no matter what our circumstances; preaching and study of the biblical text during the season of transition is no exception. Thus, focusing on what God has to say to us during this season of change is important. We can take courage from the witnesses to God's enduring presence as well as gain confidence in seeking a new direction and leadership for our ministry. God's Word shared by our own words, our own investment in one another, and our call to be a witnessing community of faith can and will strengthen and direct us on our path to the future.

> *We can take courage from the witnesses to God's enduring presence as well as gain confidence in seeking a new direction and leadership for our ministry.*

Unfortunately, not all congregations and not all temporary pastors take advantage of this reality in this seminal season. I know of a congregation who called an interim pastor who served for more than two years, simply holding the place. By that I mean there was no evidence of addressing the past or the future, no preaching from the biblical text to engage this particular moment in their seeking new leadership and direction for their church. The sermons were thoughtful and sound, but they could have been given from any pulpit on any given morning in any given church. Perhaps this is why there was no progress, no resolution to the transition. Failure to use the opportunities God gives, including the exploration of God's Word for us, limits our potential now and for the future.

Pay attention to all the transitions and leadership changes you can find in scripture; hear what they might be saying in your context, to your leadership and congregation. Consistently keeping the work of this transition season before the people is key if you want them to engage in it; ignoring the challenges won't make underlying issues go away. Expose them, investigate them, work with God to heal them, and dream God's future for you and your church. Let God's Word inform our words as we live our faithfulness together.

Takeaways

- Grounding ourselves in biblical narratives about transition will support our work as a congregation.
- The biblical text speaks of both communities and individuals in transition; these stories can inform our own.
- Scripture also talks about transformation: the opportunity to become new. We can choose just to transition or to seek transformation as we transition.
- The biblical text can and should shape our work during this season of transition, communally and individually.

Congregational Resources

Engaging the Bible for Transition and Transformation

You can engage the biblical text in a variety of ways during the pastoral transition in your church, in addition to preaching and traditional Bible study. Many of these can be intergenerational and can include people connected to your congregation but physically unable to attend. Get everyone involved! You might try one of the following:

- Pass out biblical references for transition and transformation, and ask people to briefly describe the transition/transformation they see in the text, God's response or activity in the midst of that experience, and what that teaches them about God, the nature of transition/transformation, and about themselves. Put each entry onto a PowerPoint slide and create a slide show to share at a congregational meeting, online, or in place of the sermon in worship. Depending on the context, this could be followed by small group conversations using the questions listed below in "Questions to Consider."

- Each week assign your congregation a biblical text focusing on transition or transformation. Ask people to study the text using Lectio Divina. (See appendix D.) Then invite people to share their experience and what they heard from the text in a learning-community setting or on a church blog, in a weekly emailed newsletter just for this purpose, or posted on your church website or Facebook and Instagram pages. Assign a new text the next week and continue.

- Choose several of the more dramatic accounts of transition or transformation and ask people to study them carefully, discuss them thoughtfully, and then act out the passages, literally or symbolically, as either a reflection of the text itself or in your own modern context. Have a discussion, asking each group to share what they thought was most important to convey in the text they were assigned and how that text can speak to your congregation.

- Write a prayer, a poem, or a psalm from one or more of the biblical texts on transition/transformation. Share them on your church's social media sites and in your bulletin or newsletter; read one in worship each week as "A word from the Word."

- Get your musicians involved! Write a song your congregation can learn and sing together throughout the transition season based on one of the transition/transformation texts. You can create something entirely new or write new words to a familiar tune. Have a group record it and post it on YouTube to share on social media. Sing it in worship and at congregational gatherings.

Some Biblical References to Transition

Israelites in the wilderness (Exo. 13:17ff)
Moses prepares Joshua (Num. 27:12-23; Deut. 31).
Elijah prepares Elisha (1 Kings 19; 2 Kings 2).
Eli tries to prepare his sons but fails (1 Sam. 2:13-17, 22-25).
God chooses Samuel to succeed Eli (1 Samuel 3).
John the Baptizer (Matt. 3; Mark 1:1-8; Luke 3:1-17; John 1:19-34)
Jesus sends followers after the resurrection (Mark 16:15; Luke 24:49; Matt. 28:7; Mark 16:7; Luke 24:9; John 21:17; Matt. 28:18-19; John 20:21).
Paul sends Timothy (2 Tim. 4:1-2).

Some Biblical References to Transformation

Genesis 28:16-17	Isaiah 43:18-19
Ezekiel 37:3-6	Acts 2
Romans 12:1-2	2 Corinthians 3:17
2 Corinthians 5:17	Ephesians 4:22-32

Ponder Pairings

Review the four quotes found in the "Quotes to Ponder" in Congregational Resources in chapter 4 (or others from that chapter that stand out to you) and see if you can pair them up with any of the biblical passages listed above (or others you find). Ask yourself these questions:

- Where do I see an example of this quote in the scripture?
- Who navigated transition successfully and who did not?
- What does this quote, paired with this biblical story, tell me about God? About our congregation?

Ezekiel 37:1-14: Considering Dry Bones, a Bible Study

Invite your adult learning community to consider the story of
Ezekiel and the dry bones in reference to their experience of the
time between permanent pastoral leaders. How might we discover the restoring power of God's breath bringing life to us in
this transition?

1. Begin by reading the passage aloud. Divide up the text to
   allow for more than one reader. Before the text is read,
   invite people to be listening for a word, phrase, or idea
   that captures their imagination, interest or generally
   stands out for them. It is helpful if people have a copy of
   the passage in front of them so they can follow along.
2. Ask participants to share what stood out for them, not
   explaining why, but simply noting what they heard. (This
   is a form of Lectio Divina; see appendix D.)
3. Read the passage aloud again, using one or more readers.
   Now invite people to notice what is taking place.
   - Notice that God asks Ezekiel a question: how does
     Ezekiel respond? What does this say about the proph-
     et's sense of the situation? How might Ezekiel feel both
     about himself and about what he sees before him?
   - What does God's prophecy promise? Have your group
     list the order in which these things are to happen:
     breath enters, life comes. Then sinews, flesh, skin, and
     breath again. Then life and then knowledge of God.
     Why do you think "breath" and "life" are spoken of
     twice here? What is important about "breath"? How
     does it relate to "life" in this passage?
   - Count how many times "breath" is used in the pas-
     sage. The Hebrew word for breath is *ruah*, which can
     mean "breath" or "wind" or "spirit." Ask, "What
     does this language of 'breath' tell us about God?"
   - Invite the group to pay close attention to their own
     breath for a few moments. Sitting up straight, feet
     on the floor, breathe in slowly from the belly, filling

your lungs. Hold that breath for four counts and then release it slowly. Do this several times and notice how your mind, body, and spirit respond. God, the giver of life, is our breath too.

4. Ask your group the following questions: Who or what do you relate to in this passage: the "dry bones" lying in the valley? The prophet, trying to understand what God wants of him? God, attempting to revive the dead? Why do you think you identify with this aspect of the text? Share your response with the group. Where would you place your congregation at this time? How are they represented in the story?

5. "Sinews" are the tough fibrous tissues that hold bone to bone or muscle to bone in our bodies. Ask, "If we, or our church, were the 'dry bones,' what would 'sinews' look like for us? What might hold us together? What gives us form and strength?"

6. "Flesh" refers to the soft parts of our body, like skeletal muscle. Flesh gives us shape. Ask, "What is shaping our congregation in these days of transition? What has shaped us in the past, for better or worse? What can we learn about how we want to be shaped in/for the future?"

7. "Skin" comes next in the transformation of the dry bones. Skin is the largest organ in the body; it covers our insides, offers some degree of protection. Ask, "Who or what is functioning as 'skin' in this time of transition? What does our collective 'skin' look like to us and to the world? In what way is it strong and beautiful? In what way is it injured, worn, or hurt? What might we need to do to heal our 'skin'?"

8. And finally, God offers "breath" and life again. Ask, "What new life do you hear God inviting you to, inviting our church to? What is your prayer for yourself and for our congregation in relationship to this new life?" Repeat the breathing exercise you did earlier, inviting people to experience their breath as God's breath filling and reviving them.

9. Close using the prayers that were suggested just before your last breath exercise. Remind one another that it was the same breath of God that blew transformation into the people gathered on Pentecost (Acts 2). God's breath can and will instill life in each of us and in our congregation if we hear God's Word and live.

Questions for Consideration in Transition and Transformation

If you made a collaborative PowerPoint (as suggested in the first option in "Engaging the Bible for Transition and Transformation," above), you could show it at a congregational gathering or worship and invite conversation about these questions in response. These questions could also serve as a follow-up to a sermon series or a learning community that is based on one or more of the transition/transformation texts. Adapt the questions to suit your need.

1. Which biblical example of transition resonates most with you? What about it draws you in? What can you learn about yourself, God, and this season of transition from this biblical story?

2. Which biblical example of transformation resonates most with you? What about it draws you in? What can you learn about yourself, God, and this season of transition from this biblical story? What made this situation transformational?

3. Which story of transition or transformation seems difficult to relate to? Why do you think this is the case? What do you struggle to understand, support, or believe in your own congregation's transition?

4. What gives you hope for yourself and your congregation in transition from these biblical stories? What inspires you to risk being vulnerable in order to experience transformation?

Ideas for Alternative Worship Services (for a Sunday when you don't have a pastor)

Often in the comings and goings of pastoral leaders, churches find themselves with a Sunday without pastoral leadership. You can adapt some of the ideas in this chapter or others and turn them into a worship experience; here are some ideas to get you started:

- Use a Bible study to replace the sermon. Invite members of the congregation to prepare and lead parts of your regular service, or stick to just the "essentials," such as prayer and scripture and perhaps music.
- Turn your worship into action. Begin with a call to worship and prayer and then invite people to perform a particular task on the church property or in your neighborhood. Afterward, bring people back to talk about how they experienced God or how their actions showed God. Close with prayer. You could try these ideas:
  - ▲ Divide into teams and clean various spaces in the church, preparing them to serve others and God;
  - ▲ Send people out in the surrounding neighborhood to pick up litter and to drop off flyers welcoming people to your church;
  - ▲ Set up a work project that supports another nonprofit organization in your community. Stuff envelopes for a mailing; organize food for a food pantry; sew, knit, or crochet items for a shelter; do yard work or simple chores for church members or neighbors.
- Visit a food pantry or a shelter and do a simple worship service with music and Bible readings there. Learn about their organization and how your congregation can interact in the future; pray for one another.
- Have a service of celebration and play intergenerational, noncompetitive games. Help people to learn one another's names or things you never knew about someone you thought you knew well.
- Focus your worship time on prayer, and instead of the sermon, read some of the scriptures above. Use the time

to pray in small groups and as a whole for your transition and transformation.

- Organize an outreach in your community in place of a sermon. Divide people into teams they would be willing to work on, and then meet and make plans. Bring the group back together to prayer for your efforts.

CHAPTER SIX

OFFERING

What Do We Have to "Offer"?

In many churches, the focal point of the offering in worship is money: we invite, sometimes gently command, one another to give to God the financial resources with which we have been blessed, our "tithes and offerings." Tithes means "tenth" in Hebrew, the amount of land, produce, fruit, or any other kind of income that belongs to God, according to multiple references in scripture (e.g., Genesis 28:20-22; Leviticus 27:30-32; Deuteronomy 12:5-6). An "offering" was anything else beyond the first tenth. An "offering" is a gift, given in faith that the receiver, God, will accept it and be honored by it. But offering our money is only the beginning; we are called to give our whole selves to God and to the work of God's reign. The offering in worship, then, is both the entrusting of ourselves to God and the giving over of what we have in hopes of receiving God's blessings, benefits, and grace.

Practically, in both biblical times and now, our giving is necessary to maintain buildings, pay salaries, and carry out ministry in its many forms. In some traditions, the offering is an element of worship that is seemingly downplayed, a necessary "evil" or embarrassment that reveals the church's financial need. In other traditions, the offering is indeed a more central act; much importance is placed on this moment as uniformed ushers in synchronized movement solemnly receive the gifts congregants generously offer to God. And of course, there are variations in between. In one congregation I served as pastor, we joked that the greatest act of faith on any given Sunday was when the pastor asked, "Will the ushers please come forward to receive our tithes and offerings?" and then looked around expectantly, hoping someone would jump up and grab a plate!

Attend a variety of churches and it becomes evident that in many worship services the offering has become mundane and routine. As more and more churches encourage participants to use online giving, the offering's meaning and necessity as an element of worship has become even less clear. Some congregations balk at online giving because individuals fear they will be judged if they aren't seen placing something in the plate; other congregations provide a "chit" of some sort just for that purpose so all can actively participate in physical giving. The offering has become an "intermission" to use the restroom before the sermon or to check cell phones for messages during the offertory music. Questions are emerging about how to treat this element of our worship and along with those, what it means to offer ourselves and our monetary gifts to God.

> *Everything belongs to God and is, in one way or another, returned to God; what we offer during worship is a tangible symbol of the many ways in which we demonstrate our love for and service to the Divine.*

I would argue that the offering should have a central place in our worship, no matter how one gives. The offering is our symbolic response to God, so I believe it certainly needs to be about more than money. As disciples of Jesus, we are called to offer all that we have and are as an expression of our worship. Our money is but a part of that offering; we are also called to give our lives—time, talents, intentions, hopes and dreams, hearts and minds. Everything belongs to God and is, in one way or another, returnable to God; what we offer during worship is a tangible symbol of the many ways in which we demonstrate our love for and service to the Divine. What we offer to God reflects who and what we are, and what we have garnered from the resources and blessings God has gifted to us.

The offering is also an act of trust, for God and us. Think about the gift giving you do. You take the time to choose a thoughtful gift for a friend or relative because you want them to enjoy it, to experience it as a reflection of your affection and care. You want them to use it, not just place it on a shelf (unless that's its intention!) or regift it to someone else. When we give a gift, we are trusting that our intention will be recognized and that the receiver will honor that intention by making use of the gift. In the same way, God gives to us and, in doing so, trusts that we will honor those gifts and use them to serve one another and the world. When we give the resources of our lives back to God, we are trusting that God will be pleased and blessed by our love even as we have been loved. So what do we need to offer during the season of pastoral transition? What does God desire and what can we provide for one another so that we would be open not only to receiving a blessing but in fact to be the blessing God envisions us to be?

During transition we can first offer ourselves to God as willing participants in God's ever-coming reign and as partners with God in the creation of a new vision as it begins to take shape and emerge within and among us, as people seeking to be made new. We do this when we open ourselves in prayer for this transformation in our congregation. We do this when we offer ourselves in service to the ministries of our church and community to which we know ourselves to be called. And we do this when we attend to the needs of one another in this season, creating safe spaces to be who God calls us to be, freeing one another from the past and empowering one another to discern and live into God's dream for our future, individually and as the community of Christ together. We offer one another the possibility of transformation in the love and light of Jesus.

Offering Safe Space

We know that change is difficult. People need spaces where they feel safe and supported, heard and cared for, so they can enter into change fully present to their emotional, psychological, and spiritual needs. We have said that transformation requires intentionality, and to move through this season of change with our best intent for health in the process, we must open up spaces in our communal life where people feel confident that their feelings and ideas will be respected and valued. Opportunities for honest conversation, personal reflection, and prayerful support encourage people to choose healthy ways of expressing how they are feeling in the midst of transition.

Spiritual leaders in the congregation, such as deacons or elders, may form small groups to help people process their experience. Existing groups might choose to spend a portion of each gathering discussing how people are experiencing the pastoral transition. Special groups might be established for helping people navigate the transition process, and people who are especially vulnerable—those with mental health concerns, those who have recently experienced a significant loss, those who seem to be most upset over the pastoral change, and those who are new to the congregation, for example—might be identified as persons who could benefit from the direct care and attention of a congregational support giver. This could be the transitional pastor, a counselor or therapist, or a spiritual leader in the congregation. It could also be a person with a generous heart and an ear for helpful listening. The goal is to offer care for those who need care when they need it so that everyone feels included, noticed, and attended to during the transition process.

> *The goal is to offer care for those who need care when they need it so that everyone feels included, noticed, and attended to during the transition process.*

Groups with this focus could take place over a series of weeks or monthly for a predetermined number of times. They could include a meal or refreshments; they could meet in someone's home or at the church or even at a community gathering spot, such as a coffee shop or diner. They could happen virtually. Be clear that this is not meant to be a therapeutic response, although congregations with resources to engage professional support might find it very useful for small or large groups. In whatever manner you go about it, creating safe spaces for people to work out their understanding of and response to a season of change provides compassionate, care-filled opportunities for people to see transition as a potentially positive spiritual experience and an invitation to their own transformation.

Offering Freedom

In addition to spaces where people can reflect on their transition experience, it is also important that congregations offer one another the freedom necessary to let go of the past and find new ways to engage the present and the future. Freedom is a gift God gives us to discover ourselves and the world we live in. It is a gift we can give one another as we release one another from our expectations and assumptions; it is a way to encourage each of us to learn and to grow.

Letting go of the past is essential for healthy transitions. (See chapter 1, "Call to Worship," and chapter 4, "Special Music.") Letting go doesn't mean forgetting or denigrating what has been, but rather it invites us to sift through what is valuable from the past to learn from in the present, while relinquishing any hold the past might have on the present or the future. Rather than expect that we will maintain what has been, reflection and freedom allow us to listen for how the past can inform and shape both today and the future. Freedom from the past means freedom from assumptions of not only *what* we will do but *who* will do it. It means freedom from emotional carryover; we don't need to be sad or regretful or even joyful forever! It means freedom from a theology, ideology, or organizational model that no longer fits or that the congregation has theologically or practically outgrown. It means freedom from the shadows of what was to live into the light of all that yet might be.

The offer of freedom is a gift we can give ourselves and one another.

- Can we offer our departing pastor the freedom to leave, to retire, to respond to a new call, to choose something/ someone other than us with honesty and integrity, and without imposing anger or guilt?

- Can we free ourselves from old responsibilities or positions of leadership so that others might express their gifts?
- Can we discover the freedom to welcome a new leader without feeling guilty ourselves or without finding the need to compare our new leader to past leaders?
- Can we claim the freedom to try new things and make mistakes?
- Can we claim the freedom to venture out in new ways, testing God's invitation to become someone and something new?

Offering one another freedom to think, pray, feel, respond, believe, ask, imagine, try and fail are gifts God gives us; how Christlike it is, then, when we have the wisdom and courage to give these same gifts to one another.

Offering Leadership

When a church experiences a pastoral leadership change, it is inevitable that they will experience other leadership changes as well. While a standing board may take on the task of securing temporary pastoral leadership, electing a pastoral search committee requires the commitment of people throughout the congregation willing to invest the time and energy needed for a deliberate process. It usually means they must relinquish their current responsibilities in order to fulfill this one. In addition, this is often a season when others decide to make a change; some leaders step away while others may become open to considering a role they haven't expressed interest in before. This results in additional change, but it also opens up opportunity to develop new leadership and ways of sharing the gifts God has placed among the congregation.

> *Embrace leadership fluidity as an opportunity for the Spirit to blow a holy wind in a new direction!*

Rather than seeing these shifts in leadership as a concern, celebrate these changes and ask people what gifts they have to offer God and one another during this transition season. This could be an opportune time to do a talents and gifts assessment in your congregation; an online search will uncover many prepared resources available to help you do this. Assume that people are changing and growing; just because they have always served in a particular way doesn't mean that's where their heart and energy lie in the present. As you look at the needs of the congregation during transition and make them known to the congregation, you might be surprised by who responds to offer their gifts for the present and perhaps the future.

While you are assessing leadership, it might also be time to review the number of boards and committees your congregation has and the composition of the organizational structure to make the necessary adjustments that best suit where the congregation thinks it is heading. Doing so will allow you to be ready for new pastoral leadership. Be forward thinking. You are not bound by the past. You have the freedom to experiment, revise, and try again! This process is a gift you give one another and your new pastor. Embrace leadership fluidity as an opportunity for the Spirit to blow a holy wind in a new direction! This might create just what your church and its members needed or were looking for.

Offering Understanding

Many churches in the midst of pastoral transition see members of the congregation come and go. Some will express heartbreak over the loss of the outgoing pastor; because they have tied their spiritual understanding to this person who is now leaving, they may also leave. Others will say little but slowly discontinue their involvement and eventually disappear. Others will decide to sit out the transition and wait to see what happens to the church and who the congregation will eventually call. What these departures are about is the makings of another book, but experience suggests that very little of it is actually about the departing pastor. I would suggest that in every congregation there are people who feel like they are on the margins, even if they appear to be strong in their support. I suspect their leaving isn't likely about the pastor or the church at all; it is most likely about their own spiritual dis-ease or lack of deep engagement, for whatever reason. The opportunity to leave may be what they have been waiting for. Know that this is a typical pattern. Pastoral departures provide an opportune time for people to make a change for themselves.

What can you do about it? Usually very little. But you *can* offer each one the gift of compassionate understanding. Give people who are missing a call; tell them you noticed they were absent and that you care about them. Send folks a personal note or email, or text them after a church event. Some people need to know that someone besides the departing/departed pastor knows they weren't there. Reach out with the offer to listen, to console, to care, and to wait for them to decide how to respond. Some might continue to come, and others will go. Try not to take it personally. It usually is about them, about change and how they have learned to react to it, about loss and the uncertainty of transition. You can only keep the door open, pray for them, and hope they will find their way home.

Even as some people leave, for some the season of pastoral change is the time to reengage. While generally fewer in number, these people will be interested in getting involved *because* this is a time of transition. Perhaps they didn't care for the previous leadership; maybe they are curious about what lies ahead. Regardless of who comes or goes, it is the generous and patient congregation who can offer welcome as well as release, staying connected to those who leave for as long as they allow and inviting those who return, or come for the first time, to discover their place in the new reality. The gift you can give is that of keeping the potential for relationship open as long as possible.

> *It is the generous and patient congregation who can offer welcome as well as release, staying connected to those who leave for as long as they allow and inviting those who return, or come for the first time, to discover their place in the new reality.*

Offering Possibility

Transformation comes by intentionality. To experience transformation, we must position ourselves in such a way that we are open to God's Spirit, invigorated by divine energy, and receptive to holy leading both individually and as the body of Christ. One of the most important things a congregation can offer one another is the gift of embracing change and exploring possibility. When we commit ourselves to discerning God's Spirit, when we are passionate about discovering God's call and direction for our congregation, then we will need to experiment and fail and try again! This is how we learn and, in learning, come to know ourselves, the people we serve, and God.

Cultivate a spirit of discernment. To "discern" is to see, know, or recognize in a manner other than with our eyes; it employs all our senses as well as our mental and spiritual capacity to think, intuit, feel, and understand. Cultivating a spirit of discernment opens us to viewing our reality through the eyes of God. It gives us the capacity to trust, explore, and wonder, and to see ourselves and others in ways we had not before.

> *One way to cultivate a spirit of discernment is to invite people repeatedly to pay attention to the activity of God in their own lives; help them to look for and see God.*

One way to cultivate a spirit of discernment is to invite people repeatedly to pay attention to the activity of God in their own lives; help them to look for and see God. I often ask my congregations, usually at the time of sharing congregational celebrations and concerns in worship, "Where did you notice God this week?" That question, repeated frequently, helps people identify the movement and experiences of their lives as God-revealing. When we begin to look for God, we are more likely to see God in action. Once we become aware of God's presence in our daily lives, we are more open to interpreting our experiences as being God-filled or God-directed. We begin to connect what is happening to us with God, and we can begin to notice the patterns of God's movement in our midst.

What happened to Nancy is a great example of this kind of discernment. Nancy was the chair of Christian education in a congregation that has led a community-wide vacation Bible school (VBS) for many years. Although VBS was planned and shared by other congregations, Nancy and our congregation provided the most leadership and offered the most effort year after year. So what happened when Nancy began to discern God's Spirit inviting her to do a new thing? Knowing that the other church leaders expected her to call everyone together to plan VBS, Nancy emailed the group and told them that she had a new idea to share this year, and she sketched out her plan, hoping it would capture their interest and that they would share her excitement. By the time of the meeting, it was clear that the others were not experiencing the same transformative call as Nancy, and they presented a united front against her idea. They wanted to do traditional VBS, just like they always had, and they wanted Nancy to lead it! Nancy was disheartened. Who should she listen to? The naysayers of newness who wanted things to "remain as they have always been" or God?

Pay attention to God and not to the expectations of others.

When Nancy met with me, her pastor, she was close to tears. She felt discouraged and blindsided; she "guessed" she "would have to do traditional VBS." "Do you *want* to do VBS, Nancy?" I asked. "No! I have this amazing *new* idea," she said, brightening. Nancy told me about the meeting; she felt pressured to do something she no longer felt called to do. The more we talked, the clearer her response became; when talking about VBS, Nancy's body language told the story. She sagged in the chair, her voice became quiet, and her smile disappeared. She appeared exhausted. But when, seconds later, she began to tell me her dreams for a citywide community fest, she sat up straight and her voice became animated, full of excitement and laughter, her face joyful! "Nancy, you *can't* do VBS this year," I told her. "Look at you; it's clear God is calling you to create a community fest! Let's pay attention to God and not to the expectations of others. They can do VBS, but *you* don't have to!" By sharing this conversation with me, Nancy invited me into her discernment process; I was able to help her notice the differences she exhibited when talking about each possibility and could confirm for her a sense of call to let go of the old and embark on the new.

With a sense of empowerment and freedom, Nancy emailed the group before the next meeting and told them that she was

committed to following the Spirit's lead and again invited them
to create this new event together. She also let them know that if
they were not interested, she would give them the information she
had about VBS, but she and our church would not participate. As
it turned out, they were not interested in trying something new;
and following the Spirit's lead as we understood it, Community
Fest was born. Community Fest was, and is, a wonderful, engaging intergenerational event that embodies the inclusive love and
transforming power of God in community. VBS happened with
less interest than ever before. Six months later I ran into one of
the VBS people, who asked if we were ready to join them again. I
thanked her and said, "No, we're still listening for the new things
God is calling us to be and do." Disgusted, she shook her head
and walked away.

I am grateful that Nancy listened to God inviting her to do
a new thing. She embraced vulnerability and claimed courage.
Because she discerned the movement of God in her own life, our
congregation turned their energy and resources to a new ministry
that continues to grow and engage us in new life-giving relationships. We offered ourselves to one another and our community
and became both givers and receivers. We trusted and honored
one another and God. We risked, learned things, and will try
again. Our efforts united us around a common experiment,
moved us out into our community in meaningful ways, deepened
our relationships with one another, and filled us with laughter
and joy! Offer yourself to God! And trust that God will offer a
new possibility to you and your congregation.

Takeaways

- Our offering in worship is more than just money; it is our
  giving of ourselves completely to the divine giver.
- Giving requires trust that our offering will be received and
  used wisely.
- During transition, we can offer one another many things,
  following the likeness of what God offers to us, including safe space, freedom, leadership, understanding, and
  possibility.

- Cultivating a sense that God is active in our lives opens us to ways of seeing God in all we experience.

Congregational Resources

A Prayer to Be an Offering

Holy Giver,
I am easily overwhelmed by what you offer to me.
I confess that I don't value myself or see what I offer
    as worthy in your sight.
Help me to see myself as you see me: loved, forgiven,
    redeemed.
Remind me that I reflect your image; what could be
    more desirable than that?
Fill me with the confidence of your Spirit so that I
    might believe that you want and need me.
Make me an offering of love and service to you that I
    might become a holy giver too.
Amen.

A Ritual for Creating Safe Spaces

We cannot assume safe spaces; we must create them. By doing so, we create a sacred place where God's loving compassion is a primary ingredient and where all who enter can trust they will be cared for and respected. Each time the group meets, remind participants of the space they have entered and invite their cooperation in creating a place where everyone's need for safety can be met.

Begin by establishing ground rules for the time and space you share together. The leader of the group can come with the rules listed here as a beginning point and ask for others to be added at the first meeting. In this way, participants can express their specific concerns and needs. Once your group is established, be sure to remind the members at each meeting that this is how you have decided to conduct yourselves together.

Ground Rules for Creating Safe Spaces

1. We will respect one another.
2. We will actively listen to one another.
3. We will ask questions for information and understanding, not debate.
4. We will maintain confidentiality; what is said in the group remains with the group unless there is concern that someone might harm themselves.
5. We will work to build trust with one another.
6. We will not judge one another.
7. We will seek to support one another.
8. We will encourage one another to grow.
   (Add other rules if the group desires.)

Prepare the space where the group will meet. Think about where the people who are coming will be most comfortable (what kind of seating, proximity to door or restroom, security, for example). Be sure that the space is private, with a door that can be closed. If possible, place seats in a circle so that everyone can see one another and place an unlit candle in the center on the floor or on a low table. If you are meeting virtually, send everyone a secure link to the meeting and ask them not to share it so you can limit those who participate. You might want to decide as a group how they feel about people having their video on or off during the gathering.

At the initial meeting, the leader welcomes people and then talks about creating a safe space, a place where group members can feel confident that they are included, respected, and cared for. Hand out or post on newsprint "Ground Rules for Creating Safe Spaces" and talk about each one. It is important that these are visible so people can refer to them as reminders. If you are meeting virtually, screen share the list or email it to participants. Ask if the group feels the need to add anything else. If not, the leader tells them that they will remind the group at each meeting that this is the gift the group offers to one another. Then invite the group to participate in the following ritual.

- After welcoming everyone, have the group read the ground rules aloud together. Then ask people to quiet themselves in preparation for beginning.
- Light the candle. Ask people to focus their attention on the light or to close their eyes if they feel comfortable doing so.

LEADER: We light this candle to remind us that this is sacred time, safe space. Here is a place we can be our authentic selves, speak our truth, own our mistakes, listen, learn, and begin again. Here we can talk about what matters to us and listen to what matters to one another. Here we can care for one another. Here we are safe. We offer this time to one another in the likeness of the One who offers it to us.

(Pause)

LEADER: God is in the midst of us. Let us open ourselves to God and to one another.

(And the conversation/meeting begins!)

Prayer for Freedom

Bound by the fears that threaten to overtake us;
bound by the past and its constraints;
bound by insecurity and a sense of helplessness;
bound by the limitations of our own imaginations;
bound by our selfishness and lack of faith;
we confess, O God, our need for you.

Liberate us to be the people you envision us to be—
freed to dare and to dream,
freed to embrace the present and the future,
freed to take responsibility and action,
freed to imagine the unimaginable,
freed to serve others with the love of Jesus.
We commit ourselves anew.
We are freed and loved in you. Together let us love
    and serve our God. Amen.

Assessing Our Gifts

People's gifts can be assessed in a number of ways. You may find resources from your denomination or online. And you may try the simple assessment here.

Discerning one's gifts and talents, passions and abilities is both an individual and a group activity. It is individual in that each one of us knows best how we feel about the things we can do. But it is a group activity as well; sometimes others see things in us that we fail to recognize ourselves, either because we simply are unaware it is a "gift" or because we are too shy or humble to call it out. This exercise invites both perspectives into the conversation so that each might feel the collaborative affirmation of others.

1. Begin by giving each person a piece of newsprint and asking them to put their name on the top in marker so that it can be easily seen. Read a biblical passage about gifts; here are some examples:

   > Like good stewards of the manifold grace of God, serve one another with whatever gift each of you has received. Whoever speaks must do so as one speaking the very words of God; whoever serves must do so with the strength God supplies, so that God may be glorified in all things through Jesus Christ. (1 Peter 4:10-11)

   > For as in one body we have many members, and not all the members have the same function, so we, who are many, are one body in Christ, and individually we are members of one another. We have gifts that differ according to the grace given to us: prophecy, in proportion to faith; ministry, in ministering; the teacher, in teaching; the exhorter, in exhortation; the giver, in generosity; the leader, in diligence; the compassionate, in cheerfulness. (Romans 12:4-8)

2. **Ask, "What are you good at?"** Ask each participant to contemplate their own gifts and talents; you can spark

their thinking by asking them to consider the things they do well, everything from daily chores to work requirements to recreational activities. Prompt them to write their list on their piece of newsprint. Then ask them to review the list and put a check mark (or star, plus sign, sticker, icon, etc.) next to the ones they enjoy doing.

3. **Ask, "What is it about this activity that gives satisfaction or happiness or joy?"** Invite participants to notice *why* they like doing these particular things they have marked. For example, "Why do I like to cook? Because it gives me the opportunity to be creative and to meet people's needs." Have them make a separate list of reasons they find meaning in these activities on the same paper. If there is space, ask them to hang their papers on a wall or lay them out on tables so that everyone can read them. If you are virtual, post and share them in Google Docs, giving editing permissions.

4. **Ask, "What do you notice?"** Now invite the entire group to move around the room to read and reflect on one another's papers. There is no judgment here; just take in the information presented. If members of the group know one another well, encourage them to write an affirmation on the papers of others at each point where they can recall this person sharing this gift in a meaningful way. They can use symbols or words to express their appreciation of this gift. Additionally, if they feel like there are gifts, talents, or skills that the person did not recognize, ask them to add these, with the permission of the paper's owner, to the list. If virtual, write on each other's documents in a unique color.

5. **Ask, "What can you offer?"** Have each person return to their newsprint and review the comments written there. Ask for feedback from individuals about what they learned about themselves and others. Suggest that each person consider one ongoing way they can offer their gifts to God and their community, as well as one new way, and write those on their paper. Again, ask those who are willing to share their results.

6. **"Offering Ourselves."** Close your time together by praying that God's Spirit will inspire each to identify and use their gifts for God's reign. You may invite people to take their newsprint home as a reminder, or you may want to hang them up where others can add affirmations and start their own newsprint. You might also want to keep a record (take a picture of each newsprint with a cell phone) so that you can call on these persons when the need for their gifts arises. Persons who participated online could print out their document.

Reaching Out in Understanding

Here are a few examples of notes that you can email or snail mail to people whose patterns of participation have changed due to the pastoral transition:

To someone who has stopped coming after the departure of a pastor:

Dear _____,

In a time of transition, people come and go, and it often takes a while for some to notice. We are aware that you are no longer attending our church regularly, and that concerns us. You have been a valuable part of our congregational life, and your faith community is missing you. I hope that your departure is temporary and that you will return to our life together very soon.

If there are ways we can support you during this season of change, please let us or the transitional pastor know. It's important that we support one another in the body of Christ. You can contact us directly at this number _____ or call the church office _____.

You are missed, and we are praying for your well-being as together we discern the direction of God for our church's future. Won't you join us in this effort? We hope that we will be able to worship with you again very soon.

Your family in faith,

_____

To someone who has begun coming after the departure of a pastor:

Dear _____,
We are joyful to have shared worship with you recently
and are encouraged by your presence with us. In the
midst of transition, it is important to give and receive
support from one another. We want to invite you to
(small group, Bible study, Sunday school class, etc.). For
more information about this event, contact _____.

   We are blessed by your presence and hope we will see
you again very soon!
God's richest blessings,

_____

To someone who is struggling with the idea of transition:

Dear _____,
When we struggle with life's transitions, it's helpful
to know that others care and are thinking of us. Your
church family realizes that this season of our life together
is particularly difficult for you, and because of that, we
are holding you in loving prayer. We want to remind you
that we face the uncertainty of the future with you and
that we love and serve a God who accompanies each one
of us no matter what our experience. We pray that you
will know this love in a very real way and that you will
take courage in remembering that you are not alone.

   We invite you to let us support you in ways that
matter to you. You can reach out to _____ at
_____ or to our transitional pastor, _____.
Your family of faith stands with you. God stands with
you. Together we are blessed by the enduring comfort of
the Holy Spirit, who makes us one.
In continued faith and service,

_____

Imagination Stations

Offering the chance to dream and imagine is a gift that propels people into the future. You can provide an opportunity to collect people's dreams by creating simple, accessible ways for them to express themselves as they move in and around your church building or virtual space.

Create a place where people can respond to the following statements, or ones like those below that particularly suit your congregation. You can do this by posting each one on a separate newsprint page; by making "kiosks" out of upright, painted refrigerator boxes and writing one statement on each side and placing them in a central location where people will pass by them; or by sharing documents online that people can add to and edit.

Statements That Spark Imagination

1. When I picture our congregation ten years from now, I see _____.
2. If I had $50,000 to give to ministry in our church and community, I would give it to _____.
3. If I was asked to create a new committee in our church to meet an unmet need, I would create the _____ in order to _____.
4. What I love most about our congregation is _____.
5. What our community needs most is _____.
6. If I knew they would say yes, I would ask _____ to _____.
7. I believe God wants our church to _____.
8. I have always wanted our church to try _____.
9. If our church disappeared tomorrow, what would our neighbors miss about us? _____.
10. The most transformative thing our church could do is _____.

CHAPTER SEVEN

COMMUNION

Becoming "Communion"

Communion is a hallowed moment in a worship service and in the life of a congregation. The tangible reminder of the expansive love of God and the cost of true discipleship draws us to one another and to God. In these moments when we share bread and cup, we are reminded of our fragility as humans seeking to be in relationship with God and with one another: we try, we stumble, fall and fail, but we are given the mercy and hope to begin again. However you understand what takes place in sharing Communion, this central expression of the Christian church unites us in celebrating God's redeeming love and grace as we eat and drink together.

Different Christian denominations have specialized understandings of what happens in this particular moment of worship. In some traditions, the elements themselves are believed to be transformed into the body and blood of Jesus. In others, they become symbols for the same. In some churches, Communion takes place weekly; in others, monthly. And in yet others, Communion happens quarterly or only on special occasions. There are churches who use wine and wafer; others serve grape juice and bread; some aren't particular about the specifics of the elements, assigning meaning to whatever is appropriate in the setting where it is shared. In some congregations this communal meal is referred to as "holy," and in others it is not.

Regardless of all the ways we differ, Communion is primarily a communal act. It is rarely taken alone; we share the elements and their meaning with one another, inviting God's presence among us and within. Just as this ritual is uniquely poised to communicate God's merciful love, I want to suggest that in times of transition, thoughtful care and communication with one another can become an act that is sacrificial in nature and holy in intention. When we allow ourselves to be in close proximity to one another and to God, we are indeed in communion.

> *We can become "a communion" together, a tangible expression of divine redemption, to be shared with one another and with the wider world.*

Over the years, I have often referred to my congregation as "this communion," reminding all of the sacred, grace-filled relationship that holds us in the love of God and in compassionate, intentional relationship with one another as we seek to follow Jesus. We do this best when we are authentic and open with one another, when we respect and hold one another accountable, when we are vulnerable and loving to one another, things many of us value but find challenging to put into practice.

During a season of change, being these things to and for one another is especially difficult but perhaps more important than ever. When we can share honest expectations, set healthy boundaries, and honor one another wherever we are in the process of growth and change, then we deepen our relationships with one another and reflect more clearly the love and grace of God. We can become "a communion" together, a tangible expression of divine redemption, to be shared with one another and with the wider world. As we celebrate Holy Communion in our worship and we remember Jesus' death and life anew, we also seek to let go of the old and find new life for our congregations, our "holy communions," as we seek transformation in times of transition.

Becoming Communion: Honest Expectations

It seems fairly obvious, but it is worth reminding folks that when one thing changes, little else remains the same. (See Wheatley in chapter 4, "Special Music.") The pastor's leaving kicks off a series of changes like ripples on a still pond, affecting everything from worship to pastoral care to community outreach, and touching everyone from the member with the most longevity to the first-time visitor in the pew. Because this is true, and because so much upheaval causes discomfort and uncertainty at every level of an organization, it's important simply to remind people that things will not, for a season or maybe ever, look, feel, sound or be "the same." Be clear about what people can expect and what they can't.

How quickly pastoral roles are reassigned or let go will affect how long people experience themselves as "out of sorts." Decide what is essential; if welcoming newcomers and visiting is a priority, then delegate that task to people who have gifts of hospitality and who can be trained to incorporate others. If attending the local clergy group is no longer important, then let it go, trusting that the next pastoral leader can choose to make that connection for themselves. Once you decide what needs to happen and which people, boards, or committees can attend to it, communicate with the congregation, letting them know who will do what and how to make contact. This is a wonderful opportunity for individuals to practice their gifts or to try new things! Invite persons to consider their own call to give leadership and continuity to important ministries and activities in this season. Sharing the ministry in new ways can lead to a sense of empowerment, confidence, and call. Keep reminding people of how things will now get done, and you will gain their encouragement and support.

Get comfortable with not doing some things.

Of course, not everything will get done. And that's okay. You can't take a key leader out of an organization and think everything will remain the same. (If you can, then that says something pretty significant about that leader.) Get comfortable with *not* doing some things. Not all groups will get pastoral leadership; not all activities will go on as planned. Some opportunities for representation will get missed, and some dreams will be postponed or never get off the ground. Give yourselves permission to prioritize the most important ministries and modify or let go of the rest. If a ministry is truly missed, folks will find a way to revive it. If it's not missed at all, you will have learned something about its importance to the congregation at this point in the journey. Do what you can, and don't waste time or energy on trying to act as if nothing is different. Everything is different! Giving one another permission and grace to make this adjustment can foster a deeper sense of relationship and appreciation within your congregation. It can be the seeds of creating communion, sacrificially loving and grace-filled relationships. This is a new season; embrace one another and the opportunity for change.

> *Setting boundaries during the transition period is especially important as leadership and responsibilities change.*

Becoming Communion: Healthy Boundaries for Pastoral Relationships

Healthy relationships between congregations and pastors are guided by appropriate emotional, physical, psychological, and spiritual boundaries to protect both congregations and clergy as each seeks to live in relational integrity. Setting boundaries during the transition period is especially important as leadership and responsibilities change. This is an ideal time to establish healthy ways to work and live together for the future, as well as to discard old patterns that may not maintain the boundaries necessary for all to feel safe and respected. Boundaries between the congregation and the outgoing pastor, between the congregation and the temporary pastor, and between the congregation and the new pastor all have aspects that need to be attended to.

Most denominations have a code of ethics for ministerial leaders that guide right relationships within a congregation. You can search online for a copy of the code of ethics your pastor has agreed to with your denomination or ask your region or judicatory to provide a copy. These guidelines serve to encourage personal and professional health, with concern for both the pastor and the congregation. American Baptist Churches USA has a specific code of ethics for transitional pastors as well as one for settled pastors. (See appendix C for both.)

A foundational principle in transition ministry agreed upon by experts and all major denominations is that the temporary/ transitional/intentional interim/interim pastor may not be a candidate for the settled pastoral position. (I will move forward with this argument using the term *temporary pastor* to substitute for transitional pastor/intentional interim/interim.) I know some congregations who think this statement is obvious, but I know more who think it is ridiculous! Why is this idea defended in some congregations and deemed crazy in others?

> *A foundational principle in transition ministry agreed upon by experts and all major denominations is that the temporary pastor may not be a candidate for the settled pastoral position.*

Professionals in transition ministry and denominational life see a number of reasons why making the temporary pastor permanent is problematic. One reason is that it inhibits the objectivity of the temporary pastor in moving the congregation through the transformation process if that pastor sees themselves as a potential successor to the departed pastor. The reality is that we behave differently if we have a stake in something. As a transitional pastor, I understand my job as that of holding up a mirror to a congregation and helping them see what they cannot see about themselves and their ministry, a task that doesn't always make me very popular. If I were a candidate for the open pastoral position, I might not be so quick to name what I see as problematic, especially if it might result in people voting against me.

Another reason why it is not good to hire the temporary pastor as the settled pastor is boundaries and trust. As a temporary pastor, I have had people who told me things about themselves or the church that I know they had never told anyone before. They felt free to do that because we shared an appropriate, healthy relationship, which included the assurance that in a few months or years, I would no longer be a part of their congregation. That reality freed them to be honest; I could hear their truth and then move on, taking what they confided with me. If I had stayed, it would have been awkward for both them and for me, and chances are high they would not have felt comfortable remaining in the congregation.

The potential for creating conflict, open or hidden, is another reason the temporary pastor is not eligible for the settled pastor's position. Not everyone will appreciate a transition season cut short, and hiring the temporary pastor usually results in just that. In every congregation where I have been the temporary pastor, usually about the third month people begin to ask why I can't just stay; they want to short-circuit the search process and hire me. That is flattering but inappropriate. Resist the temptation to serve short-term goals such as reducing congregational anxiety or hurrying the pastoral search. If you want the transition to be a time of transformation, you need to trust God, the process, and the work of the temporary minister for healthy change to be realized.

> *Resist the temptation to serve short-term goals such as reducing congregational anxiety or hurrying the pastoral search.*

Hiring the temporary pastor gives an unfair advantage over others who might want to be considered, another reason why this is not a wise choice. Once inside a congregation and intimately familiar with its people and history, it is difficult not to use that information for an advantage over others who are strangers but worthy pastoral candidates. Also, hiring the temporary pastor usually negates the tasks of fully exploring the congregation's past, coming to grips with the present, and imagining the future. All these things take time and thoughtful reflection. Calling the temporary pastor hijacks the transformative work of transition as well and shortcuts the pastoral search process, denying the congregation the insights each affords.

You can prevent all this by reminding the congregation repeatedly that you are blessed to have a temporary pastor whom you love; imagine how much more wonderful the person God is calling to your congregation must be! You should also include a clear statement in your contract with the temporary pastor that indicates that the temporary pastor "shall not be a candidate for the installed position." Beginning with this agreement and communicating it as often as necessary to the congregation establishes healthy boundaries with the temporary pastor and keeps the congregation on the path for transformation.

Now, what about those who think it's fine to hire the temporary pastor as the settled pastor? I'd like to think that they haven't been exposed to the potential transformation a season of transition can provide a congregation. For congregations who rely on succession ministry in its traditional form (having the departing pastor choose their successor; see chapter 1, "Call to Worship"), some of the defense of this idea is about protecting the departing pastor's legacy. By choosing who succeeds them as the temporary or settled pastor, departing pastors may hope that their work will continue and their memory will be honored, even that they can continue to actively participate in a pastoral role in some way.

While the "son," "daughter," or friend of the departing pastor may indeed be a reasonable prospect for the settled pastor's position, it is best, for both them and the congregation, to proceed through the normal course of discernment and denominational process. If they are indeed the best choice, that will be made clear at the appropriate time. Calling the temporary pastor cuts off this process and can sow discord within the congregation. Some folks are so uncomfortable with the anxiety of transition that they are willing to stop the process at any cost. Others will want to continue to discover themselves and God's prospects for pastoral leadership.

You can reassure the departing pastor of the congregation's appreciation for their ministry (if that is indeed the case) but encourage their support by allowing the freedom that a season of transition represents. The need of the departing pastor to control who serves as temporary or settled pastor is both ego-driven and fear-based; it seeks to prioritize the needs of the pastor who is leaving over those of the congregation who remains. A stronger legacy can be assured by blessing a congregation with time to assess, imagine, and experiment under the leadership of a temporary pastor as the congregation discerns God's new call.

As the temporary pastor leads the transition, healthy boundaries with the congregation are as important as the boundaries with the previous pastor. During the transition period, it is important that the previous pastor distance themselves from the congregation, even if only for this season. In some cases, this is not an issue because the previous pastor moves to another church or takes on another position, often relocating. But even so, the temptation for parishioner and pastor to continue to be in relationship is strong. The prevalence and ease of contact through social media contributes to this challenge. Remember what Bridges emphasized in chapter 4, "Special Music": good endings are the most important determinant of new beginnings. Making a clear break with a congregation is the departing pastor's professional responsibility; congregants should not make this difficult by continuing to reach out to the former pastor. A strong communion can encourage one another to respect this important boundary.

> *Departing pastors should consider this boundary an important aspect of their legacy to ensure that their congregation can make meaningful relationships with the settled pastor and continue to minister after they are gone.*

A general rule is that both the previous pastor and the temporary pastor should not have contact with the congregation for at least one year after the call of the new settled pastor. (See appendix C.) This boundary allows the congregation closure with the departing pastor and opportunity to begin to establish relationships with the new pastor. Departing pastors should consider this boundary an important aspect of their legacy to ensure that their congregation can make meaningful relationships with the settled pastor and continue to minister after they are gone. Exceptions to this guideline during the transition period should be at the discretion of the temporary pastor. Exceptions to this understanding after the arrival of the settled pastor should be negotiated between the new pastor and any previous clergy who wish to remain in the congregation.

Becoming Communion: Healthy Social Media Relationships

Let me start by admitting that I am not into much social media; I prefer my relationships face-to-face, and as both a pastor and a university professor who interfaces with many, many people, I choose to spend more time actually with them, not reading about them. But I know I am an outlier in this digital age. What do healthy social media relationships look like? In some ways, not all that different from face-to-face relationships.

Many clergy have social media accounts; what should they do when they leave a church? If they are to take the boundary-setting wisdom of stepping away from relationships with former parishioners, what does that look like on social media? The same question needs to be asked from the other perspective: How does a congregant create a healthy virtual relationship with a former pastor? These are important conversations to have as pastors and congregations take leave of one another.

When a church I belonged to lost its pastor to another position across the country, he was clear about setting little expectation that he would be involved with the church he was leaving in the near future. That would not be difficult, given he would literally be thousands of miles away. Most folks seemed to understand that meant a distance on social media as well, although it was not specifically articulated to the entire congregation. One person in particular made a point of keeping everyone else apprised of the former pastor's activities as he posted them on Facebook. She admittedly kept in contact and didn't see why that mattered since he was geographically so far away. Meanwhile the interim pastor began his work, and our "social media connector" was seemingly disconnected from that effort. It wasn't until she was asked to stop reporting on the previous pastor and encouraged to be present to the current congregational leader that she stopped—or at least became quiet about it.

Just because we can be in touch with people around the globe or in the next community, that doesn't mean we should or that it is a healthy practice to maintain at certain points in our transitional life together. Social, psychological, and emotional distancing is important for healthy endings and new beginnings, and both pastors and their congregations need to agree on what that looks like for the good of all. A pastor who has left needs space to grieve their own loss and transition into a new setting with new relationships unencumbered by those of the past. In the same way, a congregation needs to emotionally release their former pastor to become engaged in a new relationship with the temporary pastor. This happens again when the temporary pastor is replaced by the settled, permanent pastor.

> *Deciding on what those social media boundaries look like before the former pastor leaves, articulating them repeatedly in the congregation, and holding one another accountable for the good of all are important and helpful steps to take.*

Be aware: some folks will think and act as if they are the exception. Allowing them to continue contact unchecked can cause resentment in those who are "following the rules." It can also put the former pastor in the difficult position of having to reject their advances; it's not easy to have to "unfriend" another (although it is sometimes necessary and best). Deciding on what those social media boundaries look like before the former pastor leaves, articulating them repeatedly in the congregation, and holding one another accountable for the good of all are important and helpful steps to take.

So what might a healthy social media boundary look like? I recommend that the departing pastor move all their Facebook "friends" who are related to their former congregation to a specific friend group and then adjust their settings so that they do not continue to send to or receive updates from these persons. The congregation should know that this is what will happen. Helping people be clear about expectations is essential to understanding and complying.

The departing pastor might remain connected with the congregation by receiving their newsletter/checking their website, but only if it is also clear that they will not and cannot respond to what they see and hear. Continuing to engage may make the departing pastor feel better, but it can also compromise their own transition into their new life. Former pastors should be removed from general emails sent to the entire congregation, for it is no longer their responsibility to respond.

The temporary pastor should be introduced on the church's social media sites so that others will be able to identify the current acting pastor, and when that person is replaced by the settled pastor, the introductions begin again. If nothing else, it gives you something to post on social media and to attract attention to your sites, as well as the opportunity to explain how your congregation is moving through a time of transition. Again, contact with the previous pastor through social media should be very limited and should go through the current pastoral leader.

When the settled pastor has been called and in the congregation long enough to establish relationships with congregants and community, it might then be appropriate for the former pastor to relax some of the distancing boundaries, with the knowledge and agreement of the current pastor. It remains the departed pastor's responsibility to handle previous relationships with care and integrity, always with an eye to support the current pastoral leader.

We create communion when we are honest and vulnerable and also when we encourage and support one another's health and well-being. Confidence that we are all loved and valued in God's reign and that we serve God in a variety of ways and places together can strengthen our resolve to treat one another well and to live out our communion even when we are separated.

Becoming Communion: Once Again, Not Just Broken, but Broken Open

One of the gifts of Communion is the reminder of God's grace. We are forgiven; we can be made new. This potential for a new beginning is not limited to individuals; in fact, some would argue it was always meant for our corporate rebirth. It can easily be both! Accepting God's mercy for both ourselves as individuals and together as a congregation allows us to put whatever we have done or left undone behind us. It enables us to release the past in order to gain the future, a new beginning in the love and likeness of God.

As you think about Communion—"broken" body/bread—consider the difference between what is simply "broken" and what is "broken open."

A season of transition is the perfect time to grab hold of this enduring promise: every congregation can claim newness of life when they commit themselves unfailingly to discern God's call and to live into the generous mercy God has offered to us. We not only receive this gift in the celebration of the Communion we share in worship, but we can become this gift as we consider the possibilities that are inherent in change. Often it is some significant life occurrence that awakens us to the need for change: a serious illness, a near-death experience, the birth of a baby, the completion of a challenging accomplishment. A pastoral transition can be such an opportunity: a new beginning for a congregation to become all that God envisions them to be. It takes courage and requires imagination. It necessitates risk-taking and creativity.

As you think about Communion—"broken" body/bread—consider again the difference between what is simply "broken" and what is "broken open." What is broken is often of no further use; it might be repurposed or parts reused, but the manner in which it originally functioned has ended. What is broken open *reveals*; it shows what was hidden, imparts what was unknown, exposes what was secret.

In a time of transition, we can pray to be broken open, that God might reveal the Spirit that is at work in each of us. We can see this as an opportunity to discover one another, to have our gifts and talents exposed, to reveal to one another our true feelings, and to love and encourage one another in fresh ways. When a pastor leaves in turmoil or conflict, congregations can truly feel and be "broken"; but to think of oneself and one's congregation as communion means to consider rather that we are "broken open" to the redeeming power of God in our midst. As we share bread and cup, as we deepen our relationships with one another, we can embody communion, shared sacrifice and grace, in the love of Christ.

Takeaways

- Our communities can become communion, redemptive expressions of God's love and mercy to one another and the world.
- Realistic expectations can free us from a sense of being overwhelmed.
- Healthy boundaries strengthen us all.
- For a number of reasons, the temporary pastoral leader should not be called as the permanent leader.
- Healthy social media relationships support both the outgoing pastor as well as the incoming pastor and congregation.
- When we are broken, we are often discarded; when we are broken open, we are available for transformation.

Congregational Resources

Cultivating Communion

In some ways, we cannot fabricate a sense of communion in any setting; it grows organically out of meaningful interaction between people united by a common purpose. You can facilitate deeper relationships within your congregation by any number of means, some of which you likely already know and do and others you may not have considered. Use this time of transition as the bond that holds you together rather than pulls you apart.

Small groups engender deeper personal relationships. Divide your congregation into groups of six or eight people (more can be too many). You can do this by geographic location, gathering people who live near one another; by common interests (reading, golf, sewing, social justice, cooking, etc.); or even by obvious differences (young straight single plus middle-aged gay couple plus senior citizen, varying gender, race, ethnicity: whatever you have to work with).

Have each group commit to gathering for several meetings, perhaps five or six; know that focusing around a shared meal or snack is often a good way to make connections. Keep the agenda simple; you can change or adapt what I suggest here, noticing that the questions get deeper and more personal as groups continue to meet. Don't short-circuit the process of developing friendship, trust, and deeper relationship by rushing. Take your time. Only God's Spirit can create true communion among us. Notice this can all be done virtually or face-to-face.

MEETING 1. Participants introduce themselves by telling the following:

- where "home" is for them (doesn't have to be where they live but where they feel the most comfortable and alive)
- what they would love to do or be if anything were possible
- when and why they came to your church
- what questions/concerns they have about the current transition
- Pray together as a way to conclude, asking people to think about how their group might create a unique ritual to begin or end their time together. *Note:* Your ritual might be how you pray together or how you enter or leave the group: greeting one another, a nod to the virtual community, giving individual embraces, sharing a group hug, lighting a candle together, engaging in a moment of silence, blessing one another, toasting one another with well wishes with the beverage of the moment—you get the idea! Be playful and creative.

MEETING 2. Begin by reintroducing yourselves, this time sharing these things:

- a favorite place
- a time each experienced something of God
- a concern for the world
- a prayer request

Talk about your group ritual and begin to enact it. Pray together before you depart.

MEETING 3. Perhaps by now you have established a level of trust where you can ask one another questions. You might also have participants write questions on slips of paper, place them in a bowl, then randomly pick a slip to respond to. If you are virtual, you could number the questions and ask people to pick a number. Questions might be broad, as in "What do you hope for the world, and why?" or personal, "Who has been the most influential person in your life?" You might share several rounds as you converse and learn more about one another. Again, enact your ritual and pray together.

MEETING 4. Are you ready to do something together? One person could lead the group in trying their hand at something: painting, reading or writing poetry, knitting, cooking. If you are meeting virtually you would need to tell participants ahead of time so they could be prepared. Maybe you could play a game that requires teams, changing teammates and spending time with each member of your group. Consider virtual breakout rooms. Use your ritual and pray together.

MEETING 5. Your group might be ready to talk about more personal, difficult things:

- greatest challenges
- a time you felt most vulnerable
- groups or people that you find hardest to love
- questions you would like to ask God

As always, use your ritual and pray together.

MEETING 6. This might be your last "official" meeting; talk with your group about whether they want to be done or continue in some way.

- Why would they want to continue?
- What would continuing look like?
- Talk about what it means to be communion with one another. How does that look? What is essential for you to call yourselves a communion?

If this is the end of your gathering, bless and pray for one another. If your congregation allows it, you might actually share Communion with one another. If your group continues, make a plan for what happens next or what you want your next focus to be.

Setting Healthy Social Media Boundaries

Create boundaries helpful to ending old and beginning new relationships and navigating transitions by using the following guidelines.

FOR THE DEPARTING PASTOR:
- Negotiate expectations for social media boundaries between the departing pastor and the congregation.
- The departing pastor moves all former congregants to their own "friend group" on Facebook and other social media sites and adjusts settings so that nothing is sent or received from these persons.
- The departing pastor might need to remove people from their social media accounts in order to establish healthy boundaries.
- The departing pastor may choose to receive newsletters from their former congregation but should be removed from routine email lists upon departure.
- The departing pastor informs the congregation how they will handle social media accounts and what the congregation can expect.

FOR THE TEMPORARY/TRANSITIONAL PASTOR:
- Introduce the temporary pastor on the church's social media sites and include them in the email list of the congregation.
- Inform the congregation how social media boundaries will be created and maintained.
- Remove the temporary pastor from the congregation's email list when the settled pastor begins.

For the congregation:

- Respect the boundaries agreed upon by the departing pastor and the congregation.
- Move the departing pastor to a "friend group" on Facebook and other social media sites and adjust your settings so that you do not send or receive updates from them.
- Don't engage the newly settled pastor on social media sites until they have given permission to do so, and only after that pastor has begun their ministry in the congregation.

A Sample Pastoral Covenant for Either the Temporary or Settled Pastor

Pastoral covenants are loosely modeled after the covenants made between the faithful and God. Each promised to do something for the other, and they were made official by a sign. Remember God's promise to Noah after the flood (Genesis 9:8-17), Abram's covenant with God (Genesis 17:1-16), God's covenant with Mary (Luke 1:26-45), and others like these throughout the biblical text. Each was made in the context of faith, each was affirmed in a public way, each was an attempt to hear and answer to needs of the moment in faithfulness and grace-filled love. Here is a template for a pastoral agreement you might make with your temporary or settled pastor. You can change it as it is appropriate to your situation.

Pastoral Covenant

In keeping with the ethical standards of (*insert your denomination here*) ministry, and in order to set forth clearly the basic agreement between _____ (the Church) and _____ (Pastor), we agree to the following:

A Two-Way Covenant

This is a covenant agreement between two partners in ministry: the Church and the Pastor. This agreement may be terminated at any time by either the Pastor or the Church giving the other partner thirty (30) days' written notice. [*Check constitution or bylaws for appropriate amount of time.*] The Pastor will submit personal information to the _____ [*name leadership group/ person*] for appropriate criminal and child-safety background checks. The length of this agreement is open-ended. The church will provide an annual review.

Covenant Specifics

1. The Pastor will begin settled ministry with the Church on _____.

2. The Pastor will provide the following services within the boundaries of a _____-hour weekly commitment. Prioritization for use of time can be negotiated with the _____ [*name leadership group*]; the Pastor will be accountable to the _____ [*name leadership group*] for use of time.
   List the priorities of the congregation for pastoral leadership. Here are some examples. Be specific where it is appropriate, including duration or time expectations if they can be spelled out.
   - Preach, lead, and be present in worship.
   - Prepare public relations news, worship material, prayer list, and church newsletter on a regular basis in partnership with administrative assistant.
   - Provide pastoral care and membership support in partnership with auxiliary staff.
   - Have primary (but not exclusive) responsibility for weddings, funerals, dedications, etc.
   - Participate as ex-officio member of boards and committees at meetings as well as monitor others when not directly involved.
   - Give leadership for community ministry and social issues in partnership with the congregation as identified as a priority by the _____ [*name leadership group*]. Manage auxiliary staff activities.
   - Be primary point of contact for ministry.

- Offer leadership to learning-community classes and other events as available within time frame.
3. The church agrees to provide the following:
   - A salary of $ _____ paid monthly ($_____ per month)
   - $_____ of the salary ($_____ per month) will be portioned as housing allowance for the Pastor.
   - In addition, the Church will pay appropriate Social Security and retirement based on salary (retirement paid to Ministers and Missionaries Benefit Board or other plan).
   - Health insurance for _____ [*state who will be covered: Pastor, marriage partner? Family?*] will be provided by this contract and be covered by _____ [*name insurance company*]. (*Note: If the Pastor has insurance through another person or position, then the church should provide an additional benefit to support health: for example, a gym membership, cost of a spiritual director or therapist, other activities, classes, or clubs that facilitate good health.*)
   - Travel allowance at current IRS standard for reimbursement, adjusted annually
   - Reimbursement for ministry-related expenses, including travel, meals, and accommodations
   - Annual continuing education funds ($ _____)
   - Other expenses as mutually agreed on
4. The church agrees that the Pastor may take five (5) paid vacation weeks during each calendar year as approved by the _____ [*name leadership group*].
5. The Pastor is responsible to the _____ [*name group*], who will conduct a yearly review.
6. The Pastor agrees to submit documentation of travel and other ministry expenses to the church office on a monthly basis.
7. The church and the temporary pastor agree that the temporary pastor may not be a candidate for the settled pastoral position. Both agree to communicate this with the congregation. [*Use this wording if this is a covenant with a temporary/transitional pastor.*]

8. The parties to this agreement are Christians and believe that the Bible commands them to make every effort to live at peace and to resolve disputes with one another in private or within the Christian church (see Matthew 18:15-20; 1 Corinthians 6:1-8). Therefore, the parties agree that any claim or dispute arising from or related to this agreement shall be settled by biblically based mediation.

For the Church:

_____   _____
(Moderator)   (Date)

_____   _____
(Diaconate/Elders)   (Date)

_____   _____
(Pastor)   (Date)

Addendum (*As necessary; this could be an ongoing circumstance, or a one-time occurrence known at the time of hire.*)

CHAPTER EIGHT

HYMN OF EXPECTATION

When the Ending Is a New Beginning

The end of a season of transition is like the final hymn of a worship service: it is an invitation to launch ourselves into the wider world of relationship with the good news of a fresh start, the message of God's love and grace on our lips and in our hearts. As your pastoral transition comes to a close, you say goodbye to your temporary pastor, and you anticipate welcoming your newly called settled pastor. This is a joyous time of both ending and beginning in the life of a congregation.

Both endings and beginnings, as you may have come to recognize, are less moments in time as they are commitments of the mind and movements of the heart. So, as you move into this last phase of your congregation's transition, you may not be sure anything all that transformative has happened in your faith community. We don't often recognize a transformation until after it has already happened; looking back we see where we were and what we were like before today. Just because you can't see anything that looks transformative, don't assume God hasn't been or isn't still at work; a new season in your life together is about to begin. If you enter it with hope and expectation, God's work will continue within.

The final hymn of a worship service is sometimes called a "hymn of expectation." It's called this to beckon us to look beyond the words on the screen or page, beyond the music in the air, to how we can live the challenge we have heard into the world, to how we can be transformed to live God's love in and through our lives. We may not know what that looks like as we join others in a closing song, but we can aspire to embody God's call to discipleship as we prepare to move out into the world. Just as we anticipate the Spirit recreating us to express our faithfulness anew, we can anticipate transformation as the transitional season in our congregation comes to an end.

Singing Your Gratitude

Before you can welcome your newly called pastor, you must say goodbye to your transitional, temporary pastor. Depending on how long you have been together, the depth of emotional and spiritual work you have shared, and how engaged you have been in the process of this season, you may have a range of feelings to consider as you, once again, say goodbye. This relationship has likely been different from any you have had with a settled pastor; you may be uncertain about what to do or to expect. Saying goodbye to the temporary pastor signals that your transition time has come to an end, that another pastor is coming to lead the life of your faith community, and that your congregation has determined it is ready for a new season of ministry and service. These are all good things; think of it as the final song you sing together in gratitude to God.

> The departure of the temporary pastor and subsequent disconnect from your faith community frees the congregation to prepare to enter into a relationship with the pastor who is newly called.

Being intentional about saying goodbye to your temporary pastor is important. Just as you welcomed this person into your church, now it is time to formalize their leaving. Why? Because once again, the boundaries are going to shift; this pastor has served you during a very important season of your community's life, and if they have done their job well, they have helped you confront the past, embrace the present, and envision the future; they may have been present long enough to officiate at weddings and funerals, and comfort those sick and hospitalized, grieving and in crisis. They may have been helpful in holding up the mirror for your congregation to see itself as it really is, an important gift that only an "outsider" can offer. They hold the confidentiality of your members; and now it's time to let them go. Emotional boundaries once again must shift; when the departing pastor no longer has responsibility for the congregation, they should also discontinue engagement with the congregation. As was true when saying goodbye to the previous pastor, the departure of the temporary pastor and subsequent disconnect from your faith community frees the congregation to prepare to enter into a relationship with the pastor who is newly called.

Recognize your departing temporary leader during worship, perhaps with a litany of release that frees them from the responsibilities you have entrusted to them. You might bless them with a communal laying on of hands, expressing gratitude for the work they have done with and for your congregation. You could host a departing meal or reception to give people a time to say goodbye. Remember that like the final hymn that leads us out into the world, this departure is preparation for the new pastor who is coming.

Sing One More Verse

When the worship service gets long, it's always tempting to cut out a verse or two of the last hymn. In fact, I've had people question me after the fact when the service ran long, and I did not do that. While I may be tempted, I rarely will cut the last hymn; I know that I have chosen it specifically because it imparts the message I want people to leave with. If they can't remember what I've said, maybe they can carry a piece of the song with them as a reminder of their call to discipleship in the days ahead.

> *Allow two to four weeks between the departure of the temporary pastor and the first Sunday of the newly called pastor.*

After saying goodbye to the transitional pastor, you may expect to welcome the new pastor the next week. After all, you've waited a long time for this moment! I want to encourage you not to do that; don't cut the expectation short. This allows the congregation to complete their emotional leave-taking of the transitional pastor and turn their attention to fully preparing for the engagement with their new, settled pastor. While you are making this transition, invite guest preachers to fill the pulpit, do something creative in worship, ask your lay leaders to make phone calls and visits. Give yourselves space and time to let go and prepare to begin again.

The Last Verse Sung Is the First Verse Lived

The movement from the last verse of the final hymn should be a joyful, confident thrust into the world. We have "worshiped": we have been called, asked for help, heard and listened to God's Word in words, struggled with truth and feelings, and envisioned ourselves as disciples, and now we are ready for the new relationship to begin. We are ready, almost, for the new pastor to arrive! I say "almost" because your expectation needs now to shift into preparation for the new pastor's arrival.

Preparing for the newly called pastor can be an exciting time in the life of the congregation; everyone can play a part! If the pastor is moving into your community, prepare a welcome basket to help ease the transition. It can contain maps, flyers, and a list of websites and information about your community. Ask people to bring in a menu from their favorite local restaurant with a signed welcome note to personalize their contribution. Include a church directory, information about important area services like gas, electric, internet, and trash and recycling options. When I moved into my home, my first congregation gifted me with a new trash receptacle filled with cleaning supplies: sponges, soaps, disinfectants, toilet paper, and paper towels. This wonderful collection provided by members of the congregation lasted for months; each time we used something they had given, we remembered them and were blessed again by their practical thoughtfulness. If you are making an information basket, when the pastor arrives, tuck a fresh loaf of bread into the basket and take it to their home or present it in worship; this simple offering speaks volumes about a congregation's welcome and care.

Another opportunity for preparation is updating the pastor's study at the church. Depending on how long it has been since the carpet was replaced, the walls painted, the lighting and technology updated, you may have little or much work to do. It is thoughtful to ask the newly called pastor if they would like to be part of the update or renovation; their involvement can be the first project you work on together, and it is respectful to ask, not assume, what color, style of furnishings, and technology preferences reflect their sense of self and ministry, another great conversation to have at the start. What you might think is the "best" selection might not be to their taste or preference. Invite the new pastor into this process to the degree they want to be involved.

In addition to the office space itself, prepare informational items to help the new pastor get to know you and settle in. An updated church directory, a pictorial directory (you can make your own), and other important church documents all aid in orienting your new leader to your congregation. Your preparation is an important and appreciated gift of hospitality and welcome to your new leader.

> *Recognize those who have served faithfully and focus your attention on the hope and anticipation a new relationship brings.*

Planning the pastor's first Sunday with the congregation also needs to happen during this time. A joyful celebration of both the long and intentional work of the pastoral search committee and others throughout the congregation, as well as a ritual of welcoming and acknowledgment of the new pastor's leadership, is important. Recognize those who have served faithfully and focus your attention on the hope and anticipation a new relationship brings. A reception or a meal following the first worship service allows people the opportunity to introduce themselves to the pastor and the pastor to introduce themselves to the congregation. Planning can involve many, which heightens the participation and support for this important occasion. Such a gathering also serves as the emotional starting place for new relationship. Inviting members and friends of the congregation to join in the celebration provides an entry point for folks who have been distant or inactive during the transition period. Call your local news outlets and invite them to come as well; you have worked hard to get to this place. Celebrate!

Finally, as you prepare for your new pastor, you will want to update your denominational office so that they know that your search is complete—who has been called and when they begin. This will encourage the regional executives to welcome your pastor and to invite clergy in the vicinity to do the same. Likewise, you might also let pastors of neighboring churches know you have called a new pastor; they might like to reach out to welcome as well.

The hymn of expectation moves us out—out of the past, out of ourselves, out of the safety of our community—to engage God's people in the world with the good news of transformation. As your congregation prepares to enter into relationship with a new pastoral leader, may you have a sense of call and lived hope that enables you to give yourself to the new season God has prepared for you.

Takeaways

- Once again, an ending precedes a beginning; it's important to say goodbye intentionally to the temporary pastor.
- Respectful boundaries facilitate emotional closure.
- Take time between the temporary pastor and the newly called pastor to prepare physically and emotionally.
- There are many ways to prepare for your new pastor; get as many people involved as possible to share the work and heighten expectation.

Congregational Resources

A LITANY OF RELEASE FOR THE TRANSITIONAL PASTOR

During their time with the congregation, the temporary pastor has fulfilled an important role. Thus, ritualizing the end of this service to remind people that another phase of

*their transition process has come to an end and to mark
the boundaries that make for a healthy closure is helpful
for both the pastor and the congregation. You can alter
this litany to reflect the actual responsibilities your transitional pastor has accepted. The "congregational leader"
may be your moderator or another officer of the church.*

CONGREGATIONAL LEADER: We have come to this place
in our journey by God's leading and grace, and today we
are ready to release our transitional pastor [*or whatever
name you have used*] from the role and responsibilities
they have fulfilled in our congregation.

TRANSITIONAL PASTOR: While it is never easy to say
goodbye, we do so today, knowing that we part because
our work together is complete; a new pastor has been
called and a new relationship between you will soon
begin.

CONGREGATIONAL LEADER: In gratitude for your
service to God and to this congregation, we release you
from your responsibilities of preparing for and leading
worship, learning communities, Bible studies, and prayer
groups. [*Note: this list should reflect the agreement you
made with the temporary pastor at the outset of your
relationship.*] We are grateful for the ways you have
nurtured our faith and called us into service in our community and wider world.

TRANSITIONAL PASTOR: With gratitude for the opportunity to serve this community, I let go of my responsibilities for worship and nurturing your faith. I pray that God
will continue to deepen your call to discipleship and to
one another.

CONGREGATIONAL LEADER: You have been a compassionate and kind caretaker among us. We release you from
responsibility to respond to our pastoral needs, visit our
sick and aging, and preside over our major life transitions.
We are thankful for your concern for each one of us.

TRANSITIONAL PASTOR: You have entrusted me to hear your prayers, to enter your homes and hospital rooms, to walk with you amid the celebrations and sadness of your lives. I am humbled and thankful for your trust and confidence in me. I will hold your confidences always.

CONGREGATIONAL LEADER: We have been blessed by your ability to see to the details of our congregational life, to be present when needed, to represent us to the wider world. In addition, you have been our pastor, our leader, our confidant, and friend. We know that letting you go is a sign that we are ready to engage the new pastor whom God has called to serve with us. We release you to love and serve other people in other congregations, with God's help.

TRANSITIONAL LEADER: As of today, I am no longer your pastor; I have been blessed by the relationships we have formed and the friendships we have made. I will continue to pray for this congregation as it moves into relationship with a new pastor. I will listen to God's call to serve anew, with your blessing and God's help.

CONGREGATION: In gratitude to God and to you, we thank you for your pastoral leadership during this time of transition. We pray God's blessing on you and your ministry, and with our love, we release you fully as our transitional pastor [*insert whatever title you have used*].

This may be followed by a prayer, led by the congregational leader. ∎

A Prayer for Releasing the Transitional Pastor

This prayer may be used with the Litany of Release or by itself as a part of a ritual of laying on of hands by the congregation.

All Loving and Compassionate God,
as you promised blessing to Sarah and Abraham,
you have blessed us.

As you walked with the people of Israel through the wilderness and desert,
you have walked with us.
As you protected Esther in her risk-taking,
you have protected us.
As you guided magi who traveled far to find the infant Jesus,
you have guided our journey in this time of seeking.

In this season of transition, your faithfulness, O God, has
been extended and expressed in the caring pastoral
ministry of _____ [*insert transitional pastor's title and
name here*].
For their ministry among us we are grateful;
for their embodiment of the gospel we give you thanks.
As we release them from their commitment to us,
we pray your blessing on their life and ministry;
may they continue to serve you in joy and know your grace.
As we part ways today, may the blessing of your Holy Spirit
unite us in love and service for the sake of your reign on
earth. Amen.

Preparing for the New Pastor

Here are some things you can do to prepare for the arrival of your
new pastor.

1. Prepare a welcome basket.
    - a container: basket, new waste can, laundry basket, or
      plastic tote
    - maps of the area
    - coupons to local businesses
    - menus from favorite restaurants with a note of per-
      sonal recommendation
    - church directory
    - cleaning supplies
    - paper products (paper towels, toilet paper, etc.)
    - staple food items for the first few days
    - subscription to the local newspaper

- flyers for upcoming community events
- fresh fruit, vegetables*
- fresh loaf of bread*
- homemade dessert*

* *These things obviously need to be added right before presenting the basket to the new pastor.*

2. Create your own pictorial directory.

   A pictorial directory of the church members is very helpful to a new pastor. You can create your own, using a cell phone and capturing peoples' images around the church or while visiting homes. Assemble the pictures on your computer, in any number of formats, from multiple images on a page to a PowerPoint to something more like a professional directory. Be sure to add names. If you already have an updated church directory with phone numbers and postal and email addresses, this could accompany your homemade pictorial directory.

3. Update your church directory.

   An updated church directory is a must-have tool for new pastors; work at getting yours updated with the latest names, postal and email addresses, and phone numbers (including cell numbers) before the pastor arrives.

4. Gather important church documents.

   Even if you have already given your new pastor these documents in the search process, assemble them again for the pastor's church office. It's helpful to have them at hand, and the new pastor's original copies may still be packed away.

   - annual reports for the last five years
   - financial reports for the last two years
   - membership lists
   - church directory
   - lists of members of boards and committees
   - church constitution and bylaws
   - important calendar dates/events for the next six months
   - website and email log-in information
   - Wi-Fi and other passwords

- phone numbers of people available to help in the first weeks; indicate what they could be available to do (e.g., provide information about community and church)
- bulletin samples from the last two months
- recent newsletters
- parking stickers or whatever is needed for the pastor to park at the church or in the community

5. Refresh or update the pastor's study.

The pastor's office most likely will need to be updated and refreshed before the new pastor arrives. Consult with the incoming pastor whenever possible, in person or by phone. Consider their preferences concerning these items:

- desk size and placement
- flooring
- wall color
- bookcases
- furniture: chairs, tables, file cabinets, trash and recycling receptacles, etc.
- lighting needs
- desktop or laptop computer or both; PC/MAC
- printer, copier
- internet connectivity
- phones: landline, cell, or both
- security: only the pastor should have keys to their study
- signage or door plate, if necessary

CHAPTER NINE

BENEDICTION

A worship service usually closes with a benediction, a brief prayer of blessing, a wish for well-being. It can be a sending of sorts, encouraging the congregation to move into the wider community, embodying the challenge, grace, and mercy of God. While we might think of it as the end of worship, the "last word," we can also think of it as the beginning of ministry in the world, the "first word" of how followers of Jesus are to live their call in the various spheres of their individual and collective lives.

Here the benediction has the same meaning: it marks the ending of this book but only the beginning of your congregation's relationship with your new pastor. Once you've gotten to this point, you might be ready to lay aside this book until the next transitional season in your life—and you may be hoping that doesn't come too soon.

I wanted to write this book because I saw and experienced congregations without knowledge and guidance of how to proceed when their pastor announced they were leaving. As I said at the beginning, there is much literature concerning the role of the clergy in transition but little that spoke to me as a member of a congregation whose pastor has resigned. Having been the pastor who left, the pastor who arrived, the transitional pastor, and the person in the pew, I wanted to share what I've learned with you, to make your journey through this uncertain time as hopeful and empowering as possible.

I really do believe that transformation is possible in the interim time. It is the fertile soil for so much: for healing, for honest openness and self and communal revelation, for the discovering of new gifts and talents, for the letting go of what no longer serves God, and for the reign of love and peace we are called to cocreate. The "chaos" (thank you, creating God and Margaret Wheatley) of the transition season can and will, if attended to with intention and grace, give way to wonderfully energizing exploration, learning, hope, and life. You have nothing to lose and everything to gain! I have learned from other authors, other clergy, other congregations, and other transitions in my own life. I am a keen believer that there is always more to know, and I hope your experience with this work will continue to inform us both as well as those who share these seasons.

My prayer is that you will find support and encouragement, guidance and inspiration in these pages; that you and your congregation will embrace the potential of this season with the blessing of a thoughtful, trained transitional pastor who will push you, show you, love you, and call you to a season of introspection, spiritual renewal, and new life!

A Benediction for Those Being Transformed

May the creator of all things good
fashion a new spirit within you
and your congregation.

May the conqueror of death
raise you to new life today
and every day.

May the Spirit of wisdom
light the fire of transformation in your hearts
so that
you
and your congregation . . .

might be willing to lose so you can gain,
weep so you can dance,
risk so you can fail and learn,

love so you can embody
the reign of God.

May it be so. Amen.

APPENDIX A

A CONGREGATIONAL DEBRIEF[1]

The purpose of the debrief is to express our feelings through the telling of stories and reflecting on the past with the hopes of noticing God's activity in the congregation. It is also a time to defuse negative feelings by speaking truthfully to reveal who and what was life-giving as well as to identify those things that were not. This will help you to discover what you can learn from the past that may be foundational for the future and what you will want to leave behind. You must determine the time frame for "the past," but generally it is the previous pastor's tenure; go farther back if there has been no transitional work done between a short succession of pastoral leaders. The debrief is facilitated by the transitional pastor or an outside leader, and strict ground rules must be agreed to and enforced to make it productive.

A congregational debrief may be appropriate if there has been any one or more of the following:

- a pastorate of more than five years
- a departing pastor leaving because of conflict of any kind
- a departing pastor leaving because of misconduct of any kind
- a congregation who has not been able to keep pastoral leaders, or who has had a series of pastoral leaders come and go relatively quickly or in succession

- a congregation steeped in history struggling to adapt to current or changing circumstances
- a sense that there is "hidden" conflict in a congregation

LEADERSHIP. The debrief should be led by either the transitional pastor or an outsider, preferably one with strong group facilitation and listening skills (e.g., another clergyperson, a counselor or therapist).

ATTENDEES. Your goal should be to gather as many people connected with the congregation and the previous pastor as possible. This usually requires a series of personal invitations to people: phone calls with follow-up, emails, and so on. If you want to include a meal in this gathering, inviting people to bring something can ensure their participation; knowing that someone is counting on their contribution may prevent them from dropping out at the last minute.

What to Say When Inviting People

- Be clear about the purpose of a debrief: "The purpose of our congregational debrief is to discover God's activity in the life of our congregation over the last _____ years. [*Fill in the term of the departed pastor.*] By telling stories and sharing reflections, we will notice where we encountered God and recognize experiences that were life-giving to our congregation. By noticing where we did not encounter God, we can begin to identify experiences or behaviors we need to leave behind as we move into this time of transition."
- Express urgency about the need for all to come: "To be sure we have an accurate recollection of our life together, it is essential that people come. Your participation is very important."
- Tell them what *won't* happen: "This will not be a free-for-all; we will agree to ground rules at the beginning, and we are not seeking in any way to disrespect anyone. We want to tell the truth about our *own* story in a way that reveals God."

The Debrief

SETUP. If you are having a meal, eat prior to the debrief. Set up the room so that the moderator of the debrief has either newsprint or a computer and projector available for use. Newsprint is preferable because you want to use it to post ground rules and to capture what people say; having the sheets available throughout the meeting allows people to look back at what has been said and make connections, which is much more difficult on slides. It is best if this exercise can be done face-to-face but if that isn't possible, or if someone who can't be physically present wants to participate, it could be done on a virtual platform such as Zoom. I have added notes to suggest how each step might be done virtually.

Ground Rules for a Congregational Debrief

These should be written out clearly and posted so they remain in front of people throughout; you may also copy them and hand them out. If meeting virtually, email them to participants after they are agreed upon.

- Listen carefully.
- Use appropriate language.
- Use "I" messages and speak only from your own perspective.
- Refrain from debating, commenting on, or arguing about another's statement.
- Refrain from responding physically, for example, eye rolling, scoffing, or jumping up.
- Questions of clarification may be asked.
- Suggestions may be made for future consideration.
- Each speaker is asked to use an economy of words so that all who wish to speak may have the opportunity to do so.
- What is said in this setting is confidential to this setting.
- *Add any here that the group would like to suggest.*

Agenda for a Congregational Debrief

1. Welcome to all and introduction of the facilitator (if necessary)
2. Facilitator's comments
   - Presents and explains the ground rules
   - Solicits agreement from the group to follow the rules and allow the facilitator to remind the group of the rules if necessary
   - Indicates that while the details of what is said here can be considered confidential, the issues raised for further consideration as a whole will be reported on and addressed
3. Questions to guide the time of listening and sharing
   Questions are asked one at a time by the facilitator, who provides a quiet time for people to reflect/write their ideas. When people appear ready, they are invited to share their response to the question. The facilitator captures their thoughts on newsprint. After everyone has said what they want to say about the first question, the process is repeated for each of the next two questions and posted on newsprint. If doing this virtually, use a shared white board or Google Doc. Note that this is not a discussion, but a report out.
   a. What do I feel good about/grateful for as I consider the last _____ years in the life of our congregation?
   b. What do I feel bad about/resent or regret as I consider the last _____ years in the life of our congregation?
   c. Where or how do I see God revealed in this?
4. Questions for clarification
   At this point, the facilitator gives people the opportunity to ask for clarification on anything they heard or saw on the newsprint/screen.
5. Future steps
   The facilitator asks one or more questions, choosing the most appropriate:
   - What can we learn about ourselves?
   - What can we learn about God?

- What would be helpful to carry forward, in spirit or action, in light of what we have said?
- What would be helpful to leave behind, in spirit or action, in light of what we have said?
- Where do we go from here?

6. Close with prayer.

Note

1. My thanks to Rev. Dr. Stephanie Sauvé, former vice president for Academic Life and dean of the faculty, Colgate Rochester Crozer Divinity School, Rochester, New York, for teaching this process and coaching me as I have used it over the years.

APPENDIX B

FIVE FOCUS AREAS FOR TRANSITION MINISTRY[1]

Experts in the area of transition ministry (Mead,[2] Nicholson,[3] Keydel[4]) agree on **five general focus areas** for a congregation during the interim period:

1. Celebrating Our Heritage: Where We Come From

- Recalls the defining stories of a congregation's past
- Explores the past as a key to shared traditions, meaning, and values
- Allows congregations to acknowledge, grieve, and heal as necessary to move into the future
- *Without a transition*, patterns, traditions, and communal stories go unevaluated; grief and healing, if necessary, are unresolved, making new direction and new attachments more difficult.

2. Mission and Core Values: Who We Are

- Identifies current congregational values in order to articulate call and purpose (What is important to us? What are we called to do and be?)
- Assesses the demographics of age, gender, race/ethnicity, orientation, wealth, resources (inside and outside the church), and structural and spiritual life as starting points for envisioning new ministry (who we are)

- Informs the congregation about themselves in order to prepare for thinking about what is needed in a new pastoral leader (What will we need?)
- *Without a transition*, congregations presume self-awareness, operating on assumption, not fact; they reflect the past, not the present or future.

3. Leadership

- Identifies congregational leaders and how they function within the changing congregational system
- Reviews leadership and organizational needs and resources
- Explores new styles of leadership as personal and programmatic experiments, adjustments, and discovery occurs
- *Without a transition*, systems evaluation doesn't happen, skills may not match needs, old leaders remain entrenched, and new leaders have difficulty gaining access to leadership positions and finding support to serve.

4. Connections: Relationships beyond Ourselves

- Connects congregations with regional and national denominational offices for support (e.g., American Baptist Churches USA, Philadelphia Baptist Association)
- Utilizes resources to guide the transition period and equip leaders in the search process with the level of denominational support they require
- Updates communication and connecting tools (technology and communication processes, websites and web pages, social media usage, etc.)
- Recognizes local and regional relationships (e.g., organizations, agencies, schools, other congregations with whom the congregation shares ministry)
- *Without a transition*, denominational and other relationships remain static and resources for growth and change can be overlooked.

5. Envisioning the Future

- Encourages congregations to live out their core values following the direction of God's Spirit
- Invites experiments with new ministries, allowing churches to call leaders with gifts to match their vision for the future
- *Without a transition*, ministry assessment is unlikely; new ideas are pushed aside in an effort to maintain the past.

Notes

1. This section is taken from the document I wrote for the Philadelphia Baptist Association titled, "Equipped to Serve Anew: Guidelines for Pastoral Transition in the Philadelphia Baptist Association," August 2018.

2. Loren Mead, *A Change of Pastors . . . and How It Affects Change in the Congregation* (Herndon, VA: Alban Institute, 2005), 18.

3. Roger Nicholson, *Temporary Shepherds: A Congregational Handbook for Interim Ministry* (Herndon, VA: Alban Institute, 1998), 6–12.

4. John Keydel, "Focus Points and the Work of the Congregation," in *Transition Ministry Today: Successful Strategies for Churches and Pastors*, ed. Norman B. Bendroth (Lanham, MD: Rowman & Littlefield), 2014, Kindle ed.

APPENDIX C

TRANSITION MINISTRIES ABCUSA
CODE OF ETHICS

Each interim pastor serving an *Transition Ministries ABCUSA* Program is required to affirm the Codes of Ethics as presented on each side of this page: (1) "The Covenant and Codes of Ethics for Professional Church Leaders of the American Baptist Churches in the U.S.A." developed by the ABC Ministers Council and (2) the interim ministry addition to the Code of Ethics adopted by the *Transition Ministries ABCUSA* Board. Your signature below affirms your commitment to comply.

❏ I accept the Covenant and Code of Ethics for Professional Church Leaders of the American Baptist Churches in the U.S.A. (as it appears on the next page).

❏ I accept the interim ministry addition to the Code of Ethics, as related to an assignment with *Transition Ministries ABCUSA*.

- I will accept an assignment only if I am in accord with the policies and procedures of the Program.

- I will be impartial about the personality and ministry of the former pastor of the congregation I serve, while at the same time helping persons of the congregation to express, understand, and evaluate their feelings about their relationship with that pastoral leader.

- I will not consult with the Pastoral Search Committee or its members regarding potential pastoral candidates and will not promote any particular candidate for the position.

- I will maintain strong professional ties during the assignment with: (1) the staff of the *TM ABCUSA* Program,

with which I have an employee-employer relationship;
(2) the assigned church, with which I negotiate and fulfill
specific interim pastoral duties; and (3) the regional
Executive/Area Minister, who is a colleague in my interim
ministry with the church.

- I will work as a team member and colleague with the
Executive/Area Minister during the assignment, keeping in
touch with that person, providing feedback on the interim
ministry progress of the congregation, and consulting
in relation to the significant emphases I anticipate in my
ministry with the church.

- I will maintain a strong emphasis on ABC mission support
and participation by the church in ABC life.

- I will not permit the church I serve as interim pastor to
consider me as a pastoral candidate.

- Upon the completion of my assignment, I will sever my
professional relations with the church and will abstain
from professional contacts with the congregation without
the request or consent of the current pastor.

- Because I am committed to the policies of the *TM ABCUSA*
Program, I will not enter into private negotiations with
the assigned church in relation to financial remuneration
or other personal benefits.

Signed _____ Date _____

THE COVENANT AND CODE OF ETHICS
FOR PROFESSIONAL CHURCH LEADERS
OF THE AMERICAN BAPTIST CHURCHES IN THE U.S.A.

Having accepted God's call to leadership in Christ's Church, I covenant with God to serve Christ and the Church with God's help, to deepen my obedience to the Two Great Commandments: to love the Lord our God with all my heart, soul, mind and strength, and to love my neighbor as myself.

In affirmation of this commitment, I will abide by the Code of Ethics of the Ministers Council of the American Baptist Churches, and I will faithfully support its purposes and ideals. As further affirmation of my commitment, I covenant with my colleagues in ministry that we will hold one another accountable for fulfillment of all the public actions set forth in our Code of Ethics

- I will hold in trust the traditions and practices of our American Baptist Churches; I will not accept a position in the American Baptist family unless I am in accord with those traditions and practices nor will I use my influence to alienate my congregation/constituents or any part thereof from its relationship and support of the denomination. If my convictions change, I will resign my position.

- I will respect and recognize the variety of calls to ministry among my American Baptist colleagues and other Christians.

- I will seek to support all colleagues in ministry by building constructive relationships wherever I serve, both with the staff where I work and with colleagues in neighboring churches.

- I will advocate adequate compensation for my profession. I will help lay persons and colleagues to understand that professional church leaders should not expect or require fees for pastoral services from constituents they serve when these constituents are helping pay their salaries.

- I will not seek personal favors or discounts on the basis of my professional status.

- I will maintain a disciplined ministry in such ways as keeping hours of prayer and devotion, endeavoring to maintain wholesome family relationships, sexual integrity, financial responsibility, regularly engaging in educational and recreational activities for professional and personal development. I will seek to maintain good health habits.

- I will recognize my primary obligation to the church or employing group to which I have been called and will accept added responsibilities only if they do not interfere with the overall effectiveness of my ministry.

- I will personally and publicly support my colleagues who experience discrimination on the basis of gender, race, age, marital status, national origin, physical impairment, or disability.

- I will, upon my resignation or retirement, sever my professional church leadership relations with my former constituents and will not make professional contacts in the field of another professional church leader without his/her request and/or consent.

- I will hold in confidence any privileged communication received by me during the conduct of my ministry. I will not disclose confidential communications in private or public except when in my practice of ministry I am convinced that the sanctity of confidentiality is outweighed by my well-founded belief that the parishioner/client will cause imminent, life-threatening, or substantial harm to self or others, or unless the privilege is waived by those giving the information.

- I will not proselytize from other Christian churches.

- I will show my personal love for God as revealed in Jesus Christ in my life and ministry as I strive together with my colleagues to preserve the dignity, maintain the discipline, and promote the integrity of the vocation to which we have been called.

Signed _____ Date _____

APPENDIX D

LECTIO DIVINA

Lectio Divina is an ancient prayer practice that can be done individually or in a group. Its simple form invites us to hear the scripture and respond to it in a way that leads to greater illumination and deeper prayer. There are many variations on this way of reading and responding to the biblical text; here is one you can use and adapt.

1. Choose a passage of scripture for yourself or the group.
2. Invite individuals to quiet their bodies and minds as they enter into this time of reflection and prayer. Explain the process and ask people to listen for the word or phrase that speaks or stands out to them. There is no need to analyze it; just listen for it.
3. Read the passage aloud and allow for several minutes of silence.
4. Ask for people to repeat the word or phrase that stood out for them, without explanation.
5. Ask a different person to reread the passage aloud and follow this with several minutes of silence.
6. Again, ask for people to share what they heard or focused on this time.
7. Ask another voice to read the passage a third time, asking participants to consider what this passage invites them to do or be.
8. Invite people to share what they heard.
9. Close with prayer.

APPENDIX E

A TRANSITIONAL SERMON

This sermon is one in a series designed to help congregations connect their journey into transition with a biblical narrative in order to see the divine potential in themselves and this season. This particular sermon was preached in worship on the first gathering of a divided, broken congregation following the forced resignation of their pastor of several years.

Ablaze with Change
JOHN 11:17-44
Rev. Dr. Marcia B. Bailey, preaching

I received an email last Sunday morning that began, "Dear Sisters, these are challenging times; hurricanes, storms, earthquakes, wildfires, rallies, politics. The world is ablaze with change, whether we like it or not." How true! Who could have imagined all these things happening within a matter of weeks, many of them at the very same time! It's an incredibly difficult thing to face devastation, loss, and destruction. It is remarkably unsettling to live through uncertainty, dislocation, and despair. The email went on to ask us, a group of friends in faith, to pray, and as I did, I thought about you—saying goodbye to your pastor last week and beginning anew this week. Whether you like it or not, your lives are "ablaze with change," change that has landed on your doorstep. Tension, felt throughout our nation brought on by history and ideology, has come to live under your roof. Uncertainty and grief and dislocation, experienced by those who have lost so much, might pretty closely describe how some of you, who have also experienced a loss, feel today. And as I read this passage of scripture again, I began to suspect that Mary and her sister Martha, even Jesus, understood those very same feelings as well. And so that's why I chose it; change comes to us whether we like it or not.

Many of you know the story: Mary and Martha sent word to Jesus that their brother, Lazarus, was ill. They wanted him to come; they apparently had some expectation that he could do something about it. Most of us would probably say we'd drop everything and go if our being present might alter the course of another's life. But not Jesus; he deliberately stayed away.

So, we are told that when Jesus arrived, Martha came out to meet him. Apparently he was yet some distance from their home. Perhaps she wanted a few minutes alone with him. Perhaps she wanted to shield him from the mourners who had come to pay their respects and who might actually make trouble for him. In a manner that may sound accusatory, or perhaps just disconsolate, she said to him, "If you had been here, my brother would not have died." Martha believed that somehow, some way, if things had been *different,* if Jesus had come *right away,* that *maybe* Lazarus would have survived; maybe Jesus *could* have done something, anything to avert this crisis, to change the tide, to stave off death. "If you had been here . . ."

I wonder how many of *you* have been thinking, *If only . . . ,* in the last few months, weeks, days. *If only* we had said this. *If only* our pastor had done that. *If only* we knew or saw or acted or avoided, everything would be different! In the best of times we often second guess ourselves, but in a time of grief and loss, in a time of tumult and change, we easily go to that place where we have no power and no control, the place of regret, the place of powerlessness, the place of *If only.*

Let me say to you that while it is natural, the place of *If only* is not a *helpful* place to be. Don't get me wrong: looking back is important and can be very useful—that is, looking back with intent to learn and grow. But looking back with the intent to punish and blame is not the same thing. Martha's words, echoed later by her sister, Mary, don't suggest that she was at all interested in where Jesus was or what he was doing; she just wanted to know why he didn't come in time to make a difference! Jesus made an at-tempt to engage her in a theological conversation: "Your brother will rise again." But Martha wasn't ready for that; she had some *feelings* she was dealing with, and they concerned Jesus. Feelings of disappointment, feelings of regret, feelings of abandonment: *We needed you, and you didn't come!* She wasn't interested in an ideological debate.

"Your brother will rise again," he told her confidently. You *know* what that comment is like. It's like the cold consolation that those with the best intentions faultily offer when we are faced with the death of someone we love: "They are in a better place," "Their suffering is over," "It's for the best," people say. Yuck! Martha had *heard* all this already! She needed more and she *wanted* more than that from Jesus! I imagine that she was so filled with sorrow and disappointment she hardly thought twice as she parroted the response she had been giving well-wishers for days, "I know he will rise again in the resurrection on the last day." I wonder if she really wanted to say, "Come on, Jesus, take me seriously! I know 'things will get better'! I know 'everything will work out according to God's plan.' But surely *you* can do better than that!"

Platitudes like "Things will work out," "It's going to be all right," even "Well, even so, we're blessed," are things we say in times of crisis, perhaps with some hope of believing them, while in truth, what we really want is what Martha really wanted—a little divine intervention, some solid consolation, concrete evidence or proof that Jesus could or would do something, anything, to make things right again.

But it's not that easy—for her or for us. Because it seems that Jesus was talking in riddles here. He spoke of resurrection and life. But the tomb was cold. Four days was a long time. Lazarus was really, *really* dead. Jesus spoke of the dead living if we only "believe" (some translations have the word "trust"), but when the pastor is suddenly gone and the congregation is at odds with one another, and the leadership is straining to do everything they can to keep the ship upright and floating, we all just want a little divine intervention that will make it right again, bring people close again, give us comfort and assurance about the way ahead.

To her credit, tempting as it might have been, Martha, however, did not fold in on her despair. She didn't get what she wanted; things didn't go the way she'd hoped. Jesus didn't come. Lazarus was dead. And although he finally showed up, he wasn't making a lot of sense. But she remained steadfast. Martha affirmed what she could about Jesus; she believed he was the Messiah, even if she didn't quite grasp the extent of what he meant about "resurrection" and "life." Martha didn't falter, she didn't flee, but rather she returned to their home and called her sister, inviting *her* to greet their friend.

You see, it's tempting to give up! It's tempting to stay away! Martha could have sent Jesus away, dismissed him and his promises of resurrection. She could have laughed at his efforts, cried at his attempted assurances, raged at his apparent lack of compassion. But she hung in there; she left him to call her sister, generously telling Mary that Jesus was asking for her, although we have no record of that being true. It is as if she had begun to accept the change that was happening around her, whether she wanted it or not.

Interestingly enough, if *Martha* went out to meet Jesus to keep him *away* from the crowd, *Mary's* visit to him as he lingered outside the village apparently led *everyone* who was gathered right to the spot where he was. Evidently Mary had the same expectations as her sister as she repeated the same sorrowful words, "If you had been here, my brother would not have died." And as she said this, she wept, and we are told that the community wept, and then Jesus, even Jesus, wept.

Much has been said about Jesus weeping. And I wonder if you have thought about this in the midst of your own personal and congregational struggle these last days and weeks. I suspect there has been some weeping in this place. I imagine some tears may have been shed in your homes, in your meetings, as well as in your former pastor's house. Jesus *wept*. He *knew* the suffering Mary and Martha were experiencing. He understood the anguish and the pain. He knew they were heartbroken and disappointed in him. And he loved Lazarus too. "Greatly disturbed in spirit and deeply moved"—words that in the original language suggest not only grief but also anger and even fear—we are told Jesus wept. Jesus *shared* in Mary and Martha's anger, grief, and fear.

What does that mean? We could get all philosophical; we could talk theologically. But let's say this: it means that Jesus really did *get* what they were feeling; he really did share what they were going through. And not only them, but you. *You.* It means quite simply, quite amazingly, that in this season of turmoil and transition, in these moments of pain and separation, in this time of loss and uncertainty, *God gets it.* God weeps: with *you*, with your *former pastor*, with your *community of faith*. Mary wept, the community wept, and Jesus wept. He did not stand outside of the reality of the situation to judge it; he didn't bombard them with words to explain it. He didn't ignore their response to dismiss it. Rather, Jesus *entered into* their pain, their dislocation, their grief in order to transform it. "Their world was ablaze with change, whether they wanted it or not."

And *change it* is exactly what he did. Oh, I know you know the story in terms of the outcome for Lazarus, but can you *hear* it, do you *know* it, will you claim that same outcome for yourselves? Standing at the now opened tomb, Jesus, again "greatly disturbed," filled with anger and pain, commanded Lazarus, "Come out!" And we are told, "The dead man came out, his hands and feet bound with strips of cloth." Jesus said to them, "Unbind him and let him go."

What did this mean for Lazarus? What does it mean for us? For Lazarus it meant he lived again! In the very next chapter of John's Gospel he is seen eating with Jesus! It means that although he would eventually die like all of us, he got another chance; he was restored to his relationships with his sisters, his family, and his friends! What I want to ask you this morning is this: *Can* you believe that this story of death transformed into life *can be your story*—the story of you as an individual, and of you, together, as a community of faith? *Will* you dare to imagine that the weeping that lingers through this long, dark night *will be replaced* as "joy comes in the morning"? *Might* you take comfort and assurance in knowing that, although God may have seemed to be at a great distance when the going got rough, when things started to fall apart, in truth you were always in God's sight, always a part of God's plan, always held in God's intention to bring you hope and life?

People of God, make this story *your own story*, by acknowledging your grief, by honestly speaking of your disappointment, by owning your unfulfilled expectations and pain, as did Martha. Dare to venture beyond your place of mourning, leading others out of the shadows, and falling on your knees before the Divine like Mary, revealing your true heart, however broken or uncertain it may be. Make this story *your own story*, by choosing to remove the stones that cover over that which has died or has been lost or just smells bad, in order that new life might enter in. Make this story *your own story*, hear *your own name being called*, and accept the invitation to "come out" into the light and love of God's mercy anew.

My friends, "when Jesus arrived," still a long way off, grief, pain, and death were everywhere. Hearts were broken, relationships were broken, trust was broken, faith was broken. But when Jesus came, *fully came*, to be in the place where Mary and Martha lived, into the place where Lazarus was buried, things changed! Sorrow gave way to rejoicing, brokenness was transformed to healing, death was conquered by life anew! Let God come fully here, to this place, in this moment and in the next few days and weeks and months as your new life together starts to unfold.

There will be difficult days; I don't know the details of your particular story, but I have accompanied other congregations who have walked similar paths. The way is not easy; but the God who loves you and calls you into being is not far away. You can go to meet God, or God will come to you. Either way will be all right.

Hurricanes, earthquakes, fires, unrest, human discord, political distress—the "world is ablaze with change whether we want it or not." Remember that you do not face it alone. God is not far off and is coming *here* to bring new life. Amen.

———